HOW
DID
IT
ALL
BEGIN?

Also by Harold Hill—

How to Live Like a King's Kid
How to Be a Winner

HAROLD HILL

with Irene Harrell

HOW DiD iT ALL BEGiN?

Illustrated by John Lawing

Scripture quotations are from the King James version of the Holy
Bible unless otherwise identified:

TLB= The Living Bible
AP= Author's paraphrase
TAB= The Amplified Bible
TEV= Good News for Modern Man
(Today's English Version)

Library of Congress Cataloging i Publication Data
Hill, Harold, 1905.

From goo to you by way of the zoo.
Bibliography: p. 93
1. Creation   2. Evolution.   3. Coversion.

1. Harrell, Irene Burk. II. Title.
BS 651.H49   21315   75-20898
ISBN 0-88270-140-1

To the greatest folks in the world—
the young people of today.

Contents

Foreword by Wernher von Braun ix

Preface xiii

Chapters

   1. How Did It all Begin? 1
      Phony Scientists' Theories

   2. How Did It All Begin? 19
      What God Says about It

   3. But What about Fossils, Carbon Dating,
      and All That? 27

   4. Man Blows It 51

   5. Can Man Be Recycled? 65

   6. Where Do We Go from Here? 71

   7. You and the Holy Spirit 29

Appendix I: Things Apes Never Do 91

Appendix II: Bibliography on Creationism 93

Appendix III: A Few Scientific Facts 101

Foreword

Six Apollo crews have visited the moon and returned safely to earth. The Skylab astronauts have spent 171 days, 13 hours, and 14 minutes working and living in space, and all have returned hale and hearty to earth.

Why are we flying to the moon? What is our purpose? What is the essential justification for the exploration of space? The answer, I am convinced, lies rooted not in whimsy, but in the nature of man.

Whereas all other living beings seem to find their places in the natural order and fulfill their role in life with a kind of calm acceptance, man clearly exhibits confusion. Why the anxiety? Why the storm and stress? Man really seems to be the only living thing uncertain of his role in the universe; and in his uncertainty, he has been calling since time immemorial upon the stars and the heavens for salvation and for answers to his eternal questions: Who am I? Why am I here?

Astromony is the oldest science, existed for thousands of years as the only science, and is today considered the queen of the sciences. Although man lacks the eye of the night owl, the scent of the fox, or the hearing of the deer, he has an uncanny ability to learn about abstruse things like the motions of the planets, the cradle-to-the-grave cycle of the stars, and the distance between stars.

The mainspring of science is curiosity. There have always been men and women who felt a burning desire to know what was under the rock, beyond the hills, across the oceans. This restless breed now wants to know what makes an atom work, through what process life reproduces itself, or what is the geological history of the moon.

But there would not be a single great accomplishment in the history of mankind without faith. Any man who strives to accomplish something needs a degree of faith. But many people find the churches, those old ramparts of faith, badly battered by the onslaught of three hundred years of scientific skepticism. This has led many to believe that science and religion are not compatible, that "knowing" and "believing" cannot live side by side.

Nothing could be further from the truth. Science and religion are not antagonists. On the contrary, they are sisters. While science tries to learn more about the creation, religion tries to better understand the Creator.

Many men who are intelligent and of good faith say they cannot visualize God. Well, can a physicist visualize an electron? The electron is materially inconceivable and yet we use it to illuminate our cities, guide our airliners through the night skies, and take the most accurate measurements. What strange rationale makes some physicists accept the electron as real while refusing to accept God? I am afraid that, although they really do not understand the electron either, they are ready to accept it because they managed to produce a rather clumsy mechanical model of it borrowed from rather limited experience in other fields, but they wouldn't know how to begin building a model of God.

For me the idea of a creation is inconceivable without God. One cannot be exposed to the law and order of the universe without concluding that there must be a divine intent behind it all.

Some evolutionists believe that the creation is the result of a random arrangement of atoms and molecules over billions of years. But when they consider the development of the human brain by random processes within a time span of less than a million years, they have to admit that this span is just not long enough. Or take the evolution of the eye in the animal world. What random process could possibly explain the simultaneous evolution of the eye's optical system, the nervous conductors of the optical signals from the eye to the brain, and the optical nerve center in the brain itself where the incoming light impulses are converted to an image the conscious mind can comprehend?

Our space ventures have been only the smallest of steps in the vast reaches of the universe and have introduced more mysteries than they have solved. Speaking for myself, I can only say that the grandeur of the cosmos serves to confirm my belief in the certainty of a Creator.

Of course, the discoveries in astronomy, biology, physics, and even in psychology have shown that we have to enlarge the medieval image of God. If there is a mind behind the immense complexities of the multitude of phenomena which man, through the tools of science, can now observe, then it is that of a Being tremendous in His power and wisdom. But we should not be dismayed by the relative insignificance of our own planet in the vast universe as modern science now sees it. In fact God deliberately reduced Himself to the stature of humanity in order to visit the earth in person, because the cumulative effect over the centuries of millions of individuals choosing to please themselves rather than God had infected the whole planet. When God became a man Himself, the experience proved to be nothing short of pure agony. In man's time-honored fashion, they would unleash the whole arsenal of weapons against Him: misrepresentation, slander, and accusation of treason. The stage was set for a situation without parallel in the history of the earth. God would visit creatures and they would nail Him to the cross!

Although I know of no reference to Christ ever commenting on scientific work, I do know that He said, "Ye shall know the truth, and the truth shall make you free." Thus I am certain that, were He among us today, Christ would encourage scientific research as modern man's most noble striving to comprehend and admire His Father's handiwork. The universe as revealed through scientific inquiry is the living witness that God has indeed been at work.

When astronaut Frank Borman returned from his unforgettable Christmas, 1968 flight around the moon with Apollo 8, he was told that a Soviet Cosmonaut recently returned from a space flight had commented that he had seen neither God nor angels on his flight. Had Borman seen God? the reporter inquired. Frank Borman replied, "No, I did not see Him either, but I saw His evidence."

Wernher von Braun
Vice President
Engineering and Development
Fairchild Industries
Germantown, Maryland

Preface

In the beginning—WHAT?

<blockquote>
Evolution says—Goo.

The Bible says—God.
</blockquote>

Does evolution really provide the answer?

Did we actually descend from freak apes?

Were our beginnings in a sea of chemical soup?

Or in a cloud of hot gases?

And if so, who made the soup or the gases?

Or is it just possible that a Supreme Being—God Himself—carefully engineered and created the whole thing?

These are some of the questions I began asking a few years ago when I suddenly realized that what had started out as soft-headed theory—the theory of evolution—was being taught as hard fact.

It had always seemed rather weird to me that so-called scientists were willing to pin their hopes on the ramblings of a religious dreamer (Darwin's only degree was in theology) to the exclusion of all other possible alternatives. A true scientist always welcomes conflicting ideas and alternative theories, because he's looking for the truth. In this, the evolutionist does not measure up; he reveals himself as a phony scientist by having a mind that is tightly closed to any facts foreign to his beliefs. He is unteachable—a sure sign of insecurity, uncertainty, and unscientific-ness.

My business is science. Scientists who do it for money are called engineers. My clients expect me to produce results, and so do I. Therefore, I cannot afford to settle for less than the most authoritative answer; I can't afford to overlook any possible theory.

After several decades of one-sided, so-called scientific brainwashing, I decided to investigate for myself what the available evidence reveals about the whole matter of where we came from and where we're going. My search began in real earnest the day I received a book entitled, *The Harmony of Science and Scripture,* by Dr. Harry Rimmer, one of the foremost scientists of this century. It came to me from his widow with a note saying she was praying for another scientist—me—to carry on the work her husband had spent many years engaged in—the work of acquainting the world with all the facts concerning the true story of our beginnings so we could get out from under the deadly dogmatism of the evolutionists and make up our own minds about the start-up of things.

As you begin to consider my report, keep in mind a few definitions and some foundation facts:

1) What is science? Science has been defined as a "body of data" arrived at by observable, repeatable experimentation.

2) What is philosophy or religion? An intellectual

concept not subject to laboratory experiment.

3) Neither evolution nor the Bible account of creation are subject to laboratory experiment—because they are neither observable nor repeatable. Therefore, neither can be proven. They come under the heading of religion or philosophy.

4) A true scientist always examines all possible answers and all available evidence prior to making a decision or forming an opinion. The evolutionist says, "Believe like I do or you're a dummy."

Let us examine together the evidence furnished by the evolutionist on the one hand and the Bible and the *true science* on the other. At the end, make your own decision on the question, *How Did It All Begin?*

Evolution says—Goo.
The Bible says—God.
What will you say?

The Rhyme of the Ancient Cell

Protozoan is my name, I'm just a single cell.
I'm sorry that I have no proof (perhaps it's just as well)
Of my beginning, back in time, when from a glob of goo
Supposedly I started things; the end of which is YOU.

For untold centuries I thought that all was going well.
Then I became dissatisfied as just a single cell.
My fortitude, my guts and grit would stand me in good stead
I made this as my final goal: to be quadruped!

I had to take it step by step, and over centuries.
But that was nothing for I knew I'd turn out as I pleased.
Ambition surged within my cell down in my gloppy bog.
By protozoan effort I became a pollywog.

For umpteen million years or so I wriggled all about
Encumbered by my stupid tail. Then fins began to sprout.
Or was it legs I next acquired? Really, I forget.
With evolution in control, you don't know *what* you'll get!

Another million years went by (or was it three or four?)
Then I sprang from my puddle and I splatted on the shore.
(But *please* do not embarrass me with questions such as this:
"How did you change your gills for lungs? You said you were a
    FISH!")

Years later in a meadow on a prehistoric morn
I took a big jump forward and I found myself airborne.
I landed in a treetop and continued to evolve,
But there was just one problem that I couldn't seem to solve.

Could I recode my DNA for teeth and hair and tail?
(I'd have to do it somehow. Evolution must not fail!)
But I didn't have to rush it, all I had to do was wait
A couple million years or more, and all would turn out great.

My patient waiting bore much fruit as happens without fail;
I changed into a reeking ape with teeth and hair and tail.
As such I wondered sometimes as the ages came and went;
This monkey-business way of life—could it all be accident?

It was such fun to be an ape! I loved to swing from trees,
I loved to munch bananas, and I loved to scratch for fleas!
I howled at all my comrades, and I gibbered at the moon,
And little did I know that all my carefree days were doomed!

Millions of long years went past, and then a million more.
And suddenly I noticed that my tail was feeling sore!
It dropped off and my hair fell out! Old Darwin strikes again!
I was a jolly ape, but now I'd turned into a man!

Would you believe I'd started out as just a gob of goo
And changed from fish to bird to ape, and ended up as you?
That theory is, as theories go, rather odd and weird
The truth, however, is a lot less complex than you feared.

If you, then, Reader, will read on, you'll find the whole true
       story
In which there's rather less of goo and rather more of glory . . .

HAROLD HILL with Irene Harrell

HOW DID IT ALL BEGIN?

Chapter 1

How Did It All Begin?

Phony Scientists' Theories

Ever since man began, he has wondered about himself. "Where did I come from?" "How did I get here?" And he has tried to come up with a concept of the beginning of things that would satisfy his understandable curiosity.

The ancient Egyptians said their god created the Nile river. In the banks of the Nile were little white fishbait worms. There were no other creatures on earth at that time, and one day their supreme god became lonely. He decided to invent people so he would have somebody to talk to. To accomplish his purpose, he sent a flood which washed the little white worms out of the mudbank. Lo and behold, they turned into men and women. Their god wasn't lonely any more. He had plenty of people to talk to.

The ancient Babylonians had a different idea. Their supreme god, Marduk, got lonely one day, too, and dreamed up a way to have companionship. When he had dreamed long enough, he took action, puckered up, and spat upon the earth he had created. Wherever his spit lit, a man sprang up. It was a good game, so he invited the men to join him.

"Go and do likewise," Marduk said. "Make me some more people." The men got in the act, spat, and women sprang up from their spittle. Not to be left out, the women got busy, too, and the rest of creation came into being. Everything that was made was made from slobber. Not very romantic, but—

Much later, a theologian named Charles Darwin took an extended trip on the good ship *Beagle* as an amateur naturalist. The voyage lasted for five years—up and down the coast of South America, to many islands, and around the world. When he wasn't being seasick, Darwin acted like a modern Snoopy, looking into things. He practiced bird-watching, and collected a whole bunch of free samples of plants, animals, rocks, and fossils and sent them home to merrie England.

Upon his return, he stirred all the specimens around in his mind for years and years, read a few books about nature, and came up with a whole Pandora's box full of ideas, right from his very own head. He theorized that all forms of life were kissing cousins: Every living thing had descended from a common ancestor, species continually improving themselves, the weak members dying out, those fit to live surviving, the sexiest multiplying the most of all.

The biggest bombshell of his unbiblical imaginings was that man was a direct descendant of a reeking, itching, jungle baboon. Well, almost. In his *Descent of Man,* Darwin wrote:

> We do not know whether man is descended from some small species, like the chimpanzee, or from one as powerful as the gorilla.

2

Either way, Darwin made a monkey out of himself, and the evolutionists let him make monkeys out of them, too.

Now Darwin didn't pretend to be a scientist to start with. He had dropped out of med school after two years of it. Actually, Darwin never claimed his theory of evolution was a fact, and he was rather surprised to find that he had invented a new religion.

For some strange reason, even though they knew no one could prove Darwin's theory,* some so-called scientists chose to believe in evolution instead of believing God's own account of how things began. These "evolutionists" got their heads together and agreed upon a new "history" of the origin of intelligent life on earth. (Of course, they never bothered to explain where the unintelligent life came from that furnished the raw ingredients to start the whole thing.)

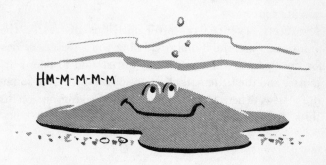

HM-M-M-M-M

---

*Even Darwin knew he could not prove his theory. In 1863, he wrote, "When we descend to details, we can prove that no one species has changed [i.e., we cannot prove that any one species has changed]; nor can we prove that the supposed changes are beneficial, which is the groundwork of the theory. Nor can we explain why some species have changed and others have not." (As quoted on page 419 of *Darwin and the Darwinian Revolution,* by Gertrude Himmelfarb. Garden City, NY: Doubleday, 1959.)

Once upon a time, they said, about four and a half billion years ago, there was a simple little cell wriggling in a swamp. (There's no such thing as a simple little cell. The single cell is one of the most complex mechanisms imaginable, but evolutionists choose to ignore that fly in their ointment.) For practically forever, the evolutionists said, the little protozoan just wriggled happily around, humming to itself in the primordial ooze, because it didn't know anything better to do. There were no Joneses to keep up with in those days, taxes were nonexistent, and it didn't *need* anything more than singing and dancing to keep itself happy.

It was a good thing little Proto was satisfied with so little for so long, because evolution requires practically forever before anything can happen. If there is a god in their system, he has to be a powerless god who can't do anything but sit back and twiddle his thumbs, waiting for nature to take its course.

Well, eventually, after millions of years, the protozoan—and the thumb-twiddling god—were rewarded for their patience. Nature finally got around to taking its course, and the little wriggling protozoan discovered something new. There were bumpy places sticking out on its sides! It had lumps!

None of the rest of the family had sprouted such adornments; little Proto had graduated to something all by himself, with no ancestral precedents to guide him. What an exciting time it was!

Everybody flocked around to observe these fascinating bulges for a few more million years—after all, there was no television, no wide-screen movies, and they had to watch *something*.

And then one day, little Proto woke up earlier than anybody else, looked lovingly down at his exclusive bulges, and saw that they had been turned into fins while he slept. Magically, though he had never seen such things before, he knew just what to do with them. He woke up the whole community with his shouts of joy.

"Hey, ma! Look! I got fins! I'm a fish! Watch me swim!"

And swim he did. Instead of just lying there in the same place all day long, slithering around in circles, little Proto shifted into high gear and swam off in search of adventure. He must have found a girl friend somewhere who liked his credentials, because after a while, the waters teemed with finned swimmers, lording it over the protozoans without lumps.

But acquired characteristics can't be passed on genetically, you argue?

Shhhh! Don't let the evolutionists hear you say that.

There is another catch, too. That is that in order for a structure to change, something must act upon it from outside to change the genetic coding of the cell. Changing the genetic coding of a cell is nothing simple, nothing that can be done with a hairpin and Scotch tape, it's a big deal, like reprogramming a fantastically complex computer. Besides that, scientists have long observed that any genetic change or mutation that sets in to make a structure more complex will destroy it sooner or later.

A mutation always represents an increase in disorder, is often sterile, and invariably a mutant is less able to cope with its surroundings than its parent was. That means that the protozoan that grew lumps would have bowed out by the second generation, simply because mutants can't make it. There is no way that a mutant could multiply and replenish the earth. (More about mutants in chapter 3.)

But evolutionists can't be bothered with such observable facts as these. Their minds are made up. Facts just confuse the issue. And so the evolutionist outwits the facts by writing his own rules as he goes along. Real scientists know that mutants usually die out, so the evolutionist authors a new *un*scientific rule which proclaims, "Mutants live longer because they are an improvement."

And so the impossible new improved protozoan with fins swims about happily until one day, after a few million more years, he notices some new lumps. They're on the bottom of him this time, not on the sides. Once again, he knows exactly what they're for.

"Hey, dad, look! I got legs! I can walk!"

He staggers up onto the land, and lo and behold, he's a lizard.

But how can he breathe? Where'd he get lungs all of a

sudden?

Don't ask me, ask the evolutionist who dreamed the whole thing up. He'll tell you the protozoan got lungs in the same place he got legs:

"He evolved them."

Anyhow, the protozoan-turned-fish has become a leaping lizard, romping around the landscape. And he has a ball for a few million years.

And then one day—you guessed it—history repeats itself, and he gets lumpy again. No, it's not adolescent acne, it's too far back for that, it must be wings!

"Hey, man, watch out! With these things, I oughta be able to take off and fly."

He backs up to get a running start, but he can't seem to get it off the ground. And for millions of years, he's a menace to navigation. His monstrous winglike appendages get in everybody's way, he falls all over himself, a big clumsy lizard with wings that won't work. But he's persistent as all get out. In his frustration, he flaps his wings so hard and long one day, they begin to fray along the edges.

"Eureka, dad! Feathers!"

Where'd the lizard get such a crazy idea as to think he could fly in the first place? Why, from his study of the principles of aerodynamics, that's where. He'd never seen anything fly. Superman comics weren't even invented yet. But he was so determined, he figured if he could just get his big hulk in fast forward motion, he could lift his landing gear and rest his feet for a change. And so, with his flap-frayed-into-feathers wings, he took a tremendous running jump— and he was suddenly airborne.

With no Civil Aeronautics regulations to tell him no-no, he could go just about anywhere he pleased. No shortage of aviation fuel, no congested airways, either. And he was so naturally fierce looking, no one even tried to hijack him anyplace. He wasn't suspect either. No airport security officer had to put on white gloves and plow through the dirty laundry in his carry-on suitcase, looking for bombs and hand guns.

Really, now. Can you imagine putting a couple of ironing boards on the sides of a Mack truck and expecting it to turn into a DC-3? It's the same principle as a big, floppy, heavy-boned, thickskinned lizard taking off into the wild blue yonder. Why, if that could happen, the government ought to revamp the museum at Kitty Hawk—make the Wright brothers move over to take second place to the first airborne lizard.

Edsel Murphy Egghead Analog Statistical Perfection—Five hundred goof-ups out of five hundred tries.

Birds are carefully engineered flying machines, not lizards with lumps. However, the evolutionists don't let that bother them. They've got a good thing going, endowed professorships all over the place, fat royalty income from fatter textbooks, pretty coeds in their classes, all kinds of fringe benefits, and so they stick with it. It's too late to turn back when you've got a vested interest established.

Somehow, during the next interim of millions of years again, the flying lizard gets tired of all that wing-beating, the glamour of being a fly-boy fades, and he decides to settle

9

Can you imagine putting a couple of ironing boards on the sides of a Mack truck and expecting it to turn into a DC-3?

down and raise a family, get his feet on the ground, you might say. So, his mind made up, he lumbers down for a beautiful five-point landing (his heavy tail was probably still standard flying lizard equipment), grows a bunch of fuzz, and turns into a monkey.

The most exciting thing of all in the whole colossal chain of events happens when a big, hairy, reeking, itching baboon in the jungle loses his hair one night. When he gets up in the morning and looks at his reflection in the swamp, he shrieks, "Good grief! I'm a people!"

And that, says the evolutionist, is where *you* came from.

To the evolutionist, it's that simple. He can actually tell it to you with a straight face. All he needs is patience and time. Given enough millions of years, anything can happen. The simple becomes the complex while he waits. Things get better by accident.

But do they really? Try an experiment—with yourself as chief guinea pig.

Let yourself go for one day.

You feel like a slob.

Let yourself go for two days.

You look like a slob.

Let yourself go for three days.

You smell like a slob.

Let yourself go for four days, and you *are* a slob. And *you* don't sprout wings—other people do, trying to get away from you.

In real life, things left to themselves run down. Fast. The garden clogs up with weeds, dust gathers on the furniture, the leftovers mold in the refrigerator. Things *never* get better by accident.

The theory of evolution flatly contradicts the backbone laws of science, the first and second laws of thermodynamics.

Edsel Murphy's Incontrovertible Laws about Things—for Eggheads:

1. If a thing can go wrong, it will—at the worst possible time.
2. If you play with a thing long enough, it will break. But don't worry. You can always do something with the pieces.
3. If a thing can go backward—it will. Watch out for the reversibility of inanimate objects.
4. Whenever you decide to do something first, something else always gets in the way.
5. You never need a thing—until after you've thrown it out and the garbage collector has picked it up.
6. It is always much harder to get out of a thing than to get into it.
7. Once a thing fouls up, whatever you do makes it worse. Except once in a while, when *it* makes *you* worse.
8. When a thing is self-explanatory, someone will want a ten-page report. With footnotes.

These laws always show up whenever and wherever things are happening—whether they're invited or not. You just can't keep them from crashing the party. In fact, they insist on running the show, and they always get their way. They must be considered wherever the action is.

The first law of thermodynamics—Thermo I—says that no one can create or destroy energy. There always is, always was, and probably there always will be the same total amount of energy—exactly one hundred percent—and that's all we have to work with. We don't worry about where it came from—we just use it. This first law of thermodynamics is also called the law of energy *conservation*.

The second law of thermodynamics, or the energy *transformation* law, says that whatever you do causes trouble. Thermo II has been called the law of increasing disorder, because it acts like a typical two-year-old. It simply gets into everything, strewing it all over the place, and when you pick up the pieces, you always end up with less than you had at the start. A contradiction of the first law? No, indeed. The portion that seems to be missing when you measure it is still around, but you can't find it. That AWOL energy is called entropy. Tired of working for a living, it has escaped to a retirement home called Unavailable Energy where it can sit incognito in a motionless rocking chair and do absolutely nothing for the rest of its days. It's of no use to anyone anymore. And because everything is made of energy, and everything that happens involves a transfer of energy, and every transfer results in some unavailable energy, eventually all energy will wind up in the rest home. When it does, the rockers will be resting, too. There'll be no available energy left to keep them in motion.

Thermo II is the reason why hot becomes cold, high becomes low, order becomes disorder, and complexity turns

13

into randomness in every known or observed energy system left to itself with no "invisible means of support." Thermo II says that eventually everything will end up in a state of heat-death, where all energy is low-grade, lukewarm, icky entropy—unavailable energy. The sun *is* cooling off, and the earth *is* slowing down measurably each year, proof of this irreversible tendency of the universe to stop happening. Thermo II would have wiped out little Proto in short order—because entropy absolutely guarantees that anything less than the simplest becomes the nothingest. Poor little Proto would have been finished off before he had a chance to develop lump number one.

Dr. Henry M. Morris, Director of the Institute for Creation Research, sums it up well in the ICR Impact Series pamphlet No. 3, entitled, "Evolution, Thermodynamics, and Entropy."

> The First Law is itself a strong witness against evolution, since it implies a basic condition of stability in the universe. . . .
>
> It is the Second Law, however, that wipes out the theory of evolution. There *is* a universal process of change, and it *is* a directional change, but it is *not* an upward change. . . . Every naturally occurring transformation of energy is accompanied, somewhere, by a loss in the *availability* of energy for the future performance of work.
>
> In this case, entropy can be expressed mathematically in terms of the total irreversible flow of heat. It expresses quantitatively the amount of energy in an energy conversion process which becomes unavailable for further work. In order for work to be done, the available energy has to "flow" from a higher level to a lower level. When it reaches the lowest level, the energy is still in existence, but no longer capable of doing work. Heat will naturally flow from a hot body to a cold body, but not from a cold body to a hot body.
>
> For this reason, no process can be 100% efficient, with

14

all of the available energy converted into work. Some must be deployed to overcome friction and will be degraded to non-recoverable heat energy, which will finally be radiated into space and dispersed. For the same reason a self-contained perpetual motion machine is an impossibility.

Since, as we have noted, everything in the physical universe is energy in some form, and since in every process, some energy becomes unavailable, it is obvious that ultimately *all* energy in the universe will be unavailable energy, if present processes go on long enough. When that happens, presumably all the various forms of energy in the universe will have been gradually converted . . . into uniformly (that is, randomly) dispersed heat energy. Everything will be at the same low temperature. There will be no "differential" of energy levels, therefore no "gradient" of energy to induce its flow. No more work can be done and the universe will reach what the physicists call its ultimate "heat death."

Thus, the Second Law proves, *as certainly as science can prove anything whatever,* that the universe had a beginning. Similarly, the First Law shows that the universe could not have begun itself. The total quantity of energy in the universe is a constant, but the quantity of *available* energy is decreasing. Therefore, as we go *backward* in time, the available energy would have been progressively greater until, finally, we would reach the beginning point, where available energy equalled total energy. Time could go back no further than this. At this point, both energy and time must have come into existence. Since energy could not create itself, the most scientific and logical conclusion to which we could possibly come is that: "In the beginning, God created the heaven and the earth."

Nice and logical, scientifically demonstrable, true. Evolutionists, however, ignore these basic laws of science and claim that with the passing of time, everything becomes better organized, more highly structured, and in better shape in an accidental sort of way. But nobody with his eyes open has ever seen it happen.

15

What do *you* see happening as you look around you?

Even though the theory of evolution has always been contrary to all the known, demonstrated laws of science, yet some egghead members of the scientific fraternity buy it as fact.

"Accidental happenings always produce accidental results," is a sound scientific statement. But evolution depends on accidental happenings, because that's what mutations are, unexpected, accidental changes in the design of living organisms.

Hillism:
A PhD without Jesus is a
Posthole Digger.

On one occasion, I understand that Darwin himself got to thinking, "If my theory of evolution is true, then it came out of the head of a freak ape, because a human being is a freak ape, a mutation. But a freak ape is not capable of making a sensible decision or coming up with a learned opinion. Therefore, my own theory has to be stupid if it's true."

That caused him some sleepless nights, I imagine. Actually, the title of one of Darwin's works hit the nail squarely on the head: *The Descent of Man,* he called it. Man has descended, all right, all the way from the superman magnificence of a Michelangelo Adam down to the sniveling sickness of the born loser of today's comic strips. But that's not the kind of "descent" Darwin had in mind. His theory of "descent" said, "Going up, please." It's a good thing Darwin wasn't an elevator operator. *Think* of the confusion!

Take your pick. I have presented three pagan concepts of the beginning of things, of the first man.

Of course, you might not like any of these concepts, preferring a history with more respectability, and ancestors more dignified than fishbait, spittoon gravy, or furry tree creatures.

In that case, there is another option open for your consideration. It's not called mythology. It's not called evolution. It's called special creation. And it says you can claim God as your Father. He tells us how it all came about in His *Manufacturer's Handbook,* the Holy Bible. And strangely enough, all that He says there is beginning to be substantiated by scientists who are interested in the facts.*

---

*See Appendix II for some Bible/Science harmonies that will blow your mind and tune you to God's wave-length.

**Egghead's Guide for Identifying
the Scientific Disciplines**

**If it stinks—it's chemistry.
If it hums—it's electricity.
If it just sits there—it's physics.
If it's green or wiggles—
it's biology.**

Chapter 2

How Did It All Begin?

What God Says about It

According to the first chapter of the *Manufacturer's Handbook,* the Holy Bible, "In the beginning, God created the heaven and the earth" (Genesis 1:1). He doesn't just tell us *that* He did it, He tells us *how* He did it. He describes the raw materials and the scientific processes by which He converted what was there in the beginning into what we know exists today.

In the beginning, "the earth was without form and void," God says, "and darkness was upon the face of the deep" (Genesis 1:2).

Prior to its transformation into matter, everything was just raw energy. It was without form and void, that is, it was invisible and empty.

Way back when I took college physics, we were taught that there was no way to transform energy into matter. "Can't be done," the eggheads told us. They also claimed the atom was the smallest particle in existence and not subject to reduction.

It's a good thing God didn't attend the same college I did. He'd have been taught that He couldn't have created the world out of the raw materials available to Him because energy couldn't be transformed into matter, according to early twentieth-century scientists. If I had been reading—and believing—the Bible in those days, I could have saved my tuition money and had all the right answers instead of the wrong ones.

All of creation was made from something invisible—energy. God says it right there in Genesis and also in the New Testament, in Hebrews 11:3: "By faith—by believing God—we know that the world and the stars—in fact, all things—were made at God's command; and that they were all made from things that can't be seen" (TLB). Pretty good hint at the atomic theory of matter, isn't it? But men were a long time at coming to understand that truth. They chose to believe their own imaginings—until the facts clobbered them over the head with the revealed truth of God.

The Bible had said for a long time that man's wisdom is foolishness to God, but my professors didn't believe that. They said, "God's wisdom is foolishness to us—we don't understand what He is saying—so we'll make up some wisdom of our own." They fed me a lot of their "wisdom," and it's taken a long time for me to get it all out of my system. Textbooks are still full of it.

When Albert Einstein came along with his amazing discovery of the relationship between energy and matter, he was in direct accord with the account of creation in the first part of Genesis. Relativity had been there from the very beginning, before mankind got around to inventing science and mathematics.

At first when Einstein said "E=MC²"
scientists shook their heads and said,
"Well, the fellow's sort of soft in the head!"

At first, when Einstein said "$E = MC^2$" (energy = mass times the speed of light squared), nobody believed him. Scientists shook their heads and said, "Well, the fellow's sort of soft in the head—roof trouble, you know. He says you can transform energy to matter at the speed of light, but we know better. Energy can't be transformed into matter. No way. It's never been done, therefore it's not possible. That's all there is to it." They closed the case—temporarily.

As things went on, however, and scientists began to learn more and more about how things *really* worked, lo and behold, they found themselves scratching their heads and saying, "You know, I believe Albert has something there. Matter of fact, from what we've been seeing in the laboratory, what he says has got to be true!"

I can just imagine God chuckling when they finally caught on. He had known it all along, from before the day when His Spirit moved and He spoke to the chaos of energy that was without form and void and said, "Let there be light." And at His Word, there was light. Energy at the speed of light (approximately 34,596,000,000 miles per second) was turned into matter, and so the world came into being.

After Einstein came along, some men began to see what God was talking about.

[Did you ever stop to think about the fact that there was light (Gen. 1:3) before the creation of the sun and the moon (Gen. 1:14-18)? That light was Jesus.* He claimed to be the Light of the world, and He was with God from the beginning (John 1:1-3). Nothing was made without Him. And if you read the next to the last chapter of the *Manufac-*

---

*Jews call Jesus by His Hebrew name, Yeshua. He is the Messiah spoken of by the prophets in the Tenach, the Hebrew Bible.

turer's Handbook, you'll see that in the New Jerusalem, Jesus, the Lamb of God, will again be the exclusive Light of the world, just as He was before the sun and moon: "And the city had no need of the sun, neither of the moon, to shine in it: for the glory of God did lighten it, and the Lamb is the light thereof " (Rev. 21:23).]

On Long Island, at the Atomic Energy Commission, there is a tremendous piece of equipment known as a cosmotron. We can introduce electromagnetic energy into it, then drop in a piece of matter, a proton, and whirl it around at a tremendous rate just under the speed of light and drop another proton in its path. The energy of the first one, plus the impact of the second upon it, produces a third one. Matter out of energy. This has been demonstrated and photographed and checked out thoroughly.*

In addition to creating matter from energy, we can change shoe leather—or any other material—into gold. In the old days, alchemists tried to change base metals to gold—and failed. Because such gold costs about half a million dollars an ounce, we don't have a very long waiting list for it, but if you've got the curiosity and the money to back it up, we can do it for you.

Today the world of science knows how to transform atomic structures. And it has advanced to the state where we can transform energy into matter, though once we were taught that not even God could do that.

In the beginning, when the Spirit of God moved (Gen. 1:2), He interfaced two gases—hydrogen and oxygen—and water appeared—H_2O. As soon as there was motion, an atom of oxygen and two atoms of hydrogen were joined in a

---

*As reported by Dr. D. Lee Chesnut, in "The Atom Speaks" and other papers (Caldwell, Idaho: Bible-Science Association).

wedding ceremony, and they became one. Water was the first molecule in creation.

Water is the backbone of life, the basic building block of man. All of us are all wet—ninety percent water.

Water is one of the most mysterious molecules we know anything about. The H_2O molecule is subject to practically no tampering. Hydrogen and oxygen appear in exclusive combination in only two forms—water (H_2O), or hydrogen peroxide (H_2O_2). Beyond that, God says, "Don't fool around, because water is basic to life."

We can take carbon and hydrogen and produce trillions of combinations—no computer yet has figured out exactly how many—but H_2O and H_2O_2 have an exclusive on their joining. No other combination can get a franchise.*

Water behaves contrary to some laws observable in the behavior of other substances. Water, as you know, is made up of a pair of gases. Ordinarily, if you heat gases, they expand; if you cool them, they contract. Most of the other gases behave like you expect them to. But water has an independent streak. When you heat water, it expands, but when you cool it, it contracts only up to a certain point, and then it begins to expand again. If it didn't, every body of water would freeze from the bottom up, and in a few hours, all the marine life—the algae and everything else—would freeze to death.

---

*Raising your eyebrows and asking, "But what about heavy water?" Yes, there is such a thing, but it doesn't wreck our argument. Heavy water is made from a heavy isotope of hydrogen called deuterium (chemical symbol D). The formula is D_2O. And because heavy water makes up only about one part in 5,000 parts of ordinary water, its contrary properties don't run the show.

A full seventy percent of our oxygen supply comes from algae in the water, so God's special arrangement for the contraction and expansion of H_2O is vital for us. It's as if He said, "Water, you must begin to expand again before you freeze solid and fall to the bottom of the pond."

God always works out special arrangements where they're needed. If He didn't, we wouldn't be here thinking about it.

Reading further along in Genesis, we see God speaking the dry land into existence (1:9) and commanding it to bring forth vegetation yielding seed *after its kind* (1:11). The animals, the fish, the birds—all of creation came into being in six days, by special creation. Last of all, God made man in His own image from the dust of the ground and breathed into him the breath of life.

If scientists can turn shoe leather into gold, it's only reasonable to believe that God could turn the dust of the ground into Adam. And He didn't have to go through a long evolutionary process, working crossword puzzles while He waited for protozoans to turn into fish, to turn into lizards, to turn into birds, to turn into monkeys, to turn into people.

Chapter 3

But What about Fossils

Carbon Dating, and All That?

"Hey, wait a minute!" I can hear some of you yelling. "But what about all the *proofs* of evolution—the fossils, carbon dating, geology, 'good' mutants, 'gill slits' in human embryos, and all that? And isn't there reliable proof that the earth is actually billions of years old instead of a few thousand years old as the Bible account would have us believe?"

Good questions, worthy of scientific answers.

First, let's look at what the evolutionists themselves have to say about the proofs of their evolutionary theories:*

---

*Quotations in this chapter are adapted from "Voices of Science on Evolution," by Prof. Robert Whitelaw, Civil Engineering Department, Virginia Polytechnic Institute, Blacksburg, Virginia, as it appeared in the *Bible-Science Newsletter* for August—September 1972, pages 8, 9, 11, and from Ray Smith's article, "The Folly of Evolution," in the August—September 1974 issue of the *Bible-Science Newsletter*.

Our first witness is Charles Darwin himself, who says, in his *Origin of the Species:*

> As by this theory, innumerable transitional forms must have existed. Why do we not find them imbedded in the crust of the earth? Why is all nature not in confusion instead of being as we see them, well-defined species? Geological research does not yield the infinitely many fine gradations between past and present species required by the theory; and this is the most obvious of the many objections which may be argued against it.

Chalk one up for honesty! Darwin admitted there was no evidence that his theory was correct. Geology was against him. Furthermore, one day he wrote:

> The horrid doubt always arises whether the convictions of man's mind, which has been developed from the mind of the lower animals, are of any value or at all trustworthy. Would anyone trust the convictions of a monkey's mind, if there are any convictions in such a mind? *(Life and Letters,* p. 285).

Darwin wasn't the only one who knew there was no evidence to support the theory of evolution but who believed in it anyway. Listen to some others:

D'Arcy Thompson, biologist, said:

> Eighty years' study of Darwinian evolution has not taught us how birds descend from reptiles, mammals from earlier quadrupeds, quadrupeds from fishes, nor vertebrates from invertebrate stock. We used to be told, and were content to believe, that the old record was of necessity imperfect. . . . But there is a deeper reason. . . . A 'principle of discontinuity' is inherent in all our classifications . . . and to seek for stepping stones across the gaps between is to seek in vain, for ever *(On Growth and Form,* p. 1093).

How about that one? Thompson acknowledges that we have *no proof*—and that we never will, even if we look forever. Le Comte du Nouy, anthropologist, wrote:

All types of reptiles appear 'suddenly' and it is impossible to link them to any terrestrial ancestors. The same is true of the tortoises. . . . We have no precise facts to go on, and no trace of intermediaries (*Human Destiny,* p. 75).

When *you* have no facts to go on, are you willing to go on without the facts? Might work for some things, but for science???

R.B. Goldschmidt, a geneticist, presents some incontrovertible facts:

Nowhere have the limits of the species been transgressed (*The Material Basis of Evolution,* p. 165, 168). Practically all orders or families known appear suddenly and without any apparent transitions ("Evolution as Viewed by One Geneticist," in the *American Scientist,* Jan. 1952, p. 97). Nobody has ever succeeded in producing a new species, not to mention the higher categories, by selection of micromutations (*Theoretical Genetics,* p. 488).

What did Goldschmidt do with the facts he found? Since they didn't uphold the theory of evolution in which he chose to believe, he bypassed the facts and said that one day a dinosaur egg must have hatched a bird.* This is called "the hopeful monster theory," but such reasoning sounds like a hope*less monstrosity* to me.

---

*Ray Smith, "The Folly of Evolution," *The Bible Science Newsletter,* August—September 1974.

George Gaylord Simpson, paleontologist, is another who failed to find the proof of evolution in nature. He admitted a deep concern over the absence of certain fossils that ought to have been found if evolution is true. But instead of rejecting evolution, he just called the missing fossils, "The major mystery of life" (*The Meaning of Evolution*). In his *The Principal Factors of Evolution,* Simpson wrote, "We do not find any continuous and progressive succession of traditional forms," and in *Science* for April 22, 1966, he said:

> Language is also the most diagnostic single trait of man; all normal men have language; no other now-living organisms do. . . . Many . . . attempts have been made to determine the evolutionary origin of language, but all have failed.

Faced with the facts against evolution, Simpson must have been embarrassed. I would have been. Loren Eiseley, anthropologist, admitted the embarrassment:

> With the failure of these many efforts [to create life] science was left in the embarrassing position of having to postulate theories of living origins which it could not demonstrate . . . of having to create a mythology of its own: namely, the assumption that what could not be proved to take place today, had, in truth, taken place in the primeval past (*Immense Journey,* p. 199).

His face still red, Eiseley, in *Scientific American* for June, 1956, stated:

> For the whole Tertiary Period . . . we have to read the story of primate evolution from a few handfuls of broken bones and teeth. These fossils, moreover, are taken from places thousands of miles apart on the Old World land mass. . . . In the end, we may shake our heads.

Edsel Murphy's Analogs
for Egghead Experimenters

1. Nothing ever works as planned. You can depend on it.
2. You never have the right amount of anything. Too little and too late, or too much and too soon. Or neither.
3. The experiment is always harder than it looks. Thank goodness. If it wasn't, you'd be without excuse for your miserable grade.
4. Never begin an experiment until after you have made up your mind how you want it to turn out.
5. If the experiment works without a hitch, you've used the wrong formula.
6. The stages of an experiment expand to exceed the time allowed. And you're supposed to clean up afterwards.
7. A laboratory collaborator is advisable. You can blame all the explosions on him.
8. Selective gravitation guarantees that toast falls buttered side down on shag rugs, jelly side up

on linoleum. But what were you doing eating in the lab?

9. Every experiment is repeatable. It should fail the same way every time. That's the exception that proves the rule.
10. Keep a careful log of results. It will prove you showed up.
11. Never talk about miracles—just depend on them.
12. Your curves will be more uniform if you draw them before your data calculation.
13. When all else fails, consult the directions. Then decide why you know an easier way.
14. The amount of equipment absolutely ruined is a fair gauge of the experience gained.
15. If a chemical reaction is slow, turn up the burner and run for your life.

Well, blushing and head-shaking may be good for something, but they don't turn up the proofs needed for evolution to be true. When Eiseley reviewed Jean Rostand's *The Orion Book of Evolution* (1961) in *The New York Times*, he must have shook his head some more:

The mutations which we know and which are considered responsible for the creation of the living world, are in general either organic deprivations, deficiencies, or the doubling of pre-existing organs. In any case, they never produce anything really new or original in the organic scheme, nothing which one might consider the basis for a new organ or the priming of a new function. . . .

No, decidedly, I cannot make myself think that these 'slips' of heredity have been able, even with the co-operation of natural selection (and) . . . immense periods of time . . . to build the entire world.

See? Evolutionists themselves admit there is plenty of evidence that mutations *can't* do what the evolutionists say they *have* to do for their own theories to be correct. James F. Crow reported, in the *Bulletin of the Atomic Scientists* for January, 1958:

Mutations and mutation rates have been studied in a wide variety of experimental plants and animals, and in man. There is one general result that clearly emerges: almost all mutations are harmful (p. 19).

For evolution to work, there must have been many marvelously good mutations, but where are they? The evolutionists can't find them. Have you seen any good mutants walking around lately?

Reviewing biochemistry professor G.A. Kerkut's book, *Implications of Evolution,* James T. Bonner wrote:

This is a book with a disturbing message; it points to some unseemly cracks in the foundations. . . . What is said gives us an uneasy feeling that we knew it for a long time but were never willing to admit this. . . . We have all been telling our students for years not to accept any statement on its face value but to examine the evidence. . . . We have failed to follow our own sound advice. (*American Scientist,* June 1961, p. 240).

When Saint Paul wrote to the church in Rome, he said, "You teach others—why don't you teach yourself?" (Romans 2:21). That might be a good question for evolutionist professors to ask themselves.

A botanist, R. Good, was getting at honesty when he acknowledged:

> There is a steadily growing realization that natural selection is not, and can never have been, the principal cause of evolution it is claimed to be. . . . It depends too much on false parallels and weakly supported assumptions (*The Listener,* May 7, 1959, p. 797).

And Alfred S. Romer, Harvard zoologist, went so far as to say:

> Below this (Cambrian strata) are vast thicknesses of sediments in which the progenitors . . . would be expected. But we do not find them; these older beds are almost barren of life, and the general picture *could reasonably be consistent with the idea of special creation.* . . . (*Natural History,* October 1959).

I bet Romer almost got excommunicated from the evolutionary fraternity for that one. In another place, he lamented:

> Links are missing just where we most fervently desire them, and it is all too probable that many 'links' will continue to be missing.

Before you get all dressed up to help Romer celebrate

with a gigantic pity-party about the missing links, take a gander at what some evolutionists did about that situation. Not satisfied with missing links, they chose to *supply* them, in some of the greatest hoaxes ever perpetrated on the "scientific" world.

I quote from Ray Smith's "The Folly of Evolution" in the August—September, 1974, issue of the *Bible-Science Newsletter* again:

Looking at exhibits in museums and at pictures in school textbooks, one would think that evolutionists had found complete skulls and skeletons of ape-men and that it is a proven fact that man ascended from the apes. Truthfully, no complete skulls or skeletons of what may honestly be called ape-men have been found. With a piece of skull, a jawbone and a few fragments, the evolutionist can produce an ape-man with all details. This is hardly honest procedure. Some of these specimens have been found to be frauds.

In 1912 near Piltdown, England, Charles Dawson and Arthur Keith discovered what they claimed was an ape-man. Sir Arthur Woodward and Teilhard de Chardin came to assist in the work. From a skull, a jawbone having teeth, and a few fragments they constructed Piltdown man which was exhibited for 41 years in the British Museum as an authentic ape-man. In 1953 John Winer and Samuel Oakley, after a long and close examination, found that the skull was of modern man, that the jawbone was that of an ape, that the teeth had been filed to look ape-like, and that the jawbone had been treated with bichromate of potassium and "salt of iron" to give it the appearance of being fossilized. . . .

E. Dubois, a Dutch surgeon, created a sensation when he announced that he had found Java man at Sumatra in Indonesia. He named it Pithecanthropus, which means ape-man. . . . After a thorough investigation, a group of German paleontologists pronounced Pithecanthropus a man, not an ape-man. Dubois admitted the remains were not those of an ape-man and that he had found remains of modern man

**Edsel Murphy Egghead Analog
Uncertainty—Rooting through the
wreckage in search of a reasonable alibi.**

in the same place.

In 1959 Dr. Louis B. Leakey announced that he had found the remains of a primitive man in Africa, and he named him Zinjanthropus. He first dated him at 600,000 years, but later (by using the Potassium/Argon method) gave him an age of more than one million years. Before his death in 1972, Dr. Leakey admitted the skull was that of an ape. In spite of these frauds, we are asked to have implicit faith in the evolutionist who is often more a philosopher than a scientist, who is sometimes in error, and sometimes is even dishonest.

Can you imagine "scientists" faking the evidence to support their shaky theories? Science is supposed to stand on fact, not on crutches of make-believe and "Let's pretend."

Hand in hand with the deceptions of the fabricators of "missing links" goes one of the weirdest science-fiction type theories still being pushed on an uninformed public. Called the "recapitulation theory," it goes something like this—

"Every human child born into this world starts out in a single-cell embryonic state, and then, through a series of changes, becomes an infant."

All okay so far. No argument. But get a load of this further rundown:

"The changes in the development of the embryo exactly duplicate all the stages represented by the Darwinian concept of protozoan-to-people, and each stage is clearly discernible in the developing embryo. The single cell changes into a fish, complete with gill slits, the fish becomes a lizard, the lizard changes into a bird, the bird into an ape, and thus into a people."

Have you swallowed all that? And doesn't it make you glad that you weren't born three months ahead of schedule? You might have wound up in the zoo with the other simians instead of in a cradle at your parents' house.

This theory, sometimes called the "biogenetic law," was dreamed up by a zoologist named Haeckel. It is still taught in many institutions of so-called higher learning. "Ontogeny (the development of an organism) recapitulates phylogeny (the evolution of a group of organisms)," Haeckel said. Some eggheads still believe him, even though all the facts point in another direction, and even the *Encyclopedia Britannica* admits that Haeckel was "somewhat unscrupulous in his treatment of scientific facts" (1970 ed., v. 10, p. 1105). Let's look at what one scientist says about Haeckel's "evidence:"

> Probably one of the most widespread of the recapitulation fallacies concerns the fact that at a particular stage of development, the human embryo possesses (as do the embryos of many mammals) structures which superficially resemble the gills of fish. These embryonic features, erroneously referred to as "gill pouches" or "gill slits," are then said to "repeat or recapitulate a fish stage in our evolution."
>
> However, this is most certainly not the case. It is true that a series of five alternating ridges and grooves are present in mammalian embryos in approximately the same region as the gill bars of aquatic vertebrates such as fish. In fish these grooves open into the pharynx, forming the true gill slits through which water passes for respiration. In mammals, birds, and reptiles, however, these structures never function in respiration, nor are there ever any openings into the pharynx. Moreover, in mammals these pharyngeal bars (as they are more properly termed) begin immediately to un-

dergo further development. . . . The first arch and its pouch [i.e., groove] . . . form the upper and lower jaws and inner ear of higher vertebrates. The second, third, and fourth arches contribute to the tongue, tonsils, parathyroid gland, and thymus.

None of these structures, it may be noted, are associated with respiration. Thus, the use of the biogenetic "law" to support the fish ancestry of mammals and other non-aquatic vertebrates has no basis in fact ("Perpetuation of the Recapitulation Myth," by Glen W. Wolfrom, *Creation Research Society Quarterly*, March 1975, p. 199).

So-called gill slits proving that people came from fish? Makes about as much sense as saying that candy canes come from zebras. Only suckers would buy reasoning like that.

If the evolutionists themselves express doubts that their case could hold up in court, and even stoop to the deceit of inventing false evidence, what do the *real* scientists say, the men who carefully examine and consider all the true evidence—pro and con—before reaching a conclusion? Just as you would expect, they find the evolutionists guilty of gross stupidity, blindness, and conclusions not supported by any facts, only by figments of their imaginations. Listen fast to a few *real* scientists:

"If the human eye came by chance, then so could a telescope!" (William Paley, famous naturalist, 1743-1805).

"The theories of evolution with which our studious youth have been deceived, constitute a dogma that all the world continues to teach; but each man in his specialty, the zoologist or the botanist, ascertains that none of the explanations furnished is adequate" (Paul Lemoine, in *Encyclopedie Francaise*, V, 82-83, 1937).

"Natural selection, contrary to what Darwin held, has a conserving effect, and *limits* the variability of species" (Emile

Guyenot, in *Encyclopedie Francaise,* V, pp. 82-83, 1937).

"It is impossible for scientists any longer to agree with Darwin's theory of the origin of species. After forty years, no evidence has been discovered to verify his genesis of species. . . .Even time cannot complete that which has not yet begun" (Sir William Bateson, famous geneticist, 1921).

"No matter how far back we go in the fossil record . . . we find no trace of any animal forms intermediate between the major groups or phyla. . . . It is a fair supposition that there never have been any such intergrading types.

"There is not the slightest evidence that any of the major groups of animals arose from each other. Each is a special animal complex . . . appearing, therefore, as a special distinct creation" (Austin H. Clark, U.S. Museum of Natural History, in *The New Evolution: Zoogenesis,* pp. 189-196).

"The most unexpected part of the paleontological evidence remains to be mentioned: the further back we look for early man, the more like ourselves he appears to be" (Dr. Rendle Short, surgeon, in *The Victoria Institute,* p. 10).

"The facts . . . do not support the notion of a beast-like early man" (M.F.A. Montagy, renowned anthropologist, in *Introduction to Physical Anthropology*).

"My attempt to demonstrate evolution by an experiment carried on for more than forty years, has completely failed. . . . It is not even possible to make a caricature of an evolution out of paleo-biological facts. The fossil material is now so complete that . . . the lack of transitional series cannot be explained as due to the scarcity of the material. The deficiences are real, they will never be filled. The idea of evolution rests on pure belief!" [Heribert Nilsson, Director of Botany Inst., Lund Univ., in *Synthetische Artbildung,* Vol. I & II, 1953 (transl.)].

"Extreme evolutionism in its various forms is an obstacle to scientific progress, because it leads those who hold it to misconceive their problems and misinterpret the data they observe. If biology is to advance, this theory should be abandoned even as a working hypothesis" (G.H. Duggan, philosopher, in *Evolution & Philosophy*).

"As we know, there is a great divergence of opinion among biologists, not only about the causes of evolution but even about the actual process. This divergence exists because the evidence is unsatisfactory and does not permit any certain conclusion. . . . We now know that the variations determined by environmental changes . . . regarded by Darwin as the material on which natural selections acts—are not hereditary. . . . The success of Darwinism was accompanied by a decline in scientific integrity. The modern Darwinian paleontologists are obliged, just like their predecessors and like Darwin, to water down the facts with subsidiary hypotheses which are in the nature of things unverifiable" (W.R. Thompson, Director, Commonwealth Inst. of Biological Control, in his introduction to *The Origin of Species*, Everyman's Library Edition, E.P. Dutton & Co., 1956).

"The probability of life originating from accident is comparable to the probability of the unabridged dictionary resulting from an explosion in a printing shop" (Edwin Conklin, biologist, Princeton Univ., in *Reader's Digest*, Jan. 1963).

"To the unprejudiced, the fossil record of plants is in favor of special creation" (E.J.H. Corner, botanist, Cambridge Univ., in *Contemporary Botanical Thought*).

"Mutations deal only with changes in existing characters, never with the appearance of a new functioning character. . . . And yet it is the appearance of new characters in organisms which marks the boundaries of the major steps in

The probability of life originating from accident is comparable to the probability of an unabridged dictionary resulting from an explosion in a printing shop.

the evolutionary scale" (H. Graham Cannon, in *The Evolution of Living Things*).

"All of our experience shows that contrary to what Darwin believed, the variability potential of each species is definitely limited" (Walter E. Lammerts, Director of Research, Germain's Horticultural Research Division, in *Discoveries Since 1859 Which Invalidate the Evolution Theory*, Creation Research Society Annual, 1964).

"Scientists who go about teaching that evolution is a fact of life are great con men, and the story they are telling may be the greatest hoax ever. In explaining evolution, we do not have one iota of fact" (T.N. Tahmisian, physiologist, Atomic Energy Commission, U.S.).

"Protoplasm evolving a universe is a superstition more pitiable than paganism" (President Leavitt of Lehigh University).

A summary of evidence against evolution is presented by George F. Howe:

"1. Complex forms often appear before simpler ones. 2. 'Advanced' and 'primitive' characters occur in the same plant. 3. Modern forms are often identical to remote fossil specimens. 4. Where phylogenies (family trees) are postulated, significant gaps occur. 5. Characters thought to belong to one group are found distributed in other unrelated groups. 6. Angiosperm [flowering plant] ancestry has remained a complete mystery" (George F. Howe, biologist, in *Paleobotanical Evidences for a Philosophy of Creationism*, Creation Research Society Annual, 1964).

"The various evidences which evolutionists cite to support their religion can be understood equally well, in fact better, in terms of creation. For example, those evidences based on superficial resemblances, such as comparative anatomy, embryo development, blood sera, and the like,

42

give strong testimony not to evolutionary kinships, but rather to their creation by a common Designer who used similar structures and patterns to accomplish similar . . . functions.

"The fossil record of former life on earth has essentially the same great unbridged gaps between the basic kinds of creatures that exist in the modern world. There is thus no genuine evidence of evolution at all!" (Henry M. Morris, hydrologist, in *Evolution, the Established Religion of the State*).

The list of credible quotations could go on and on. There is no proof that evolution is true, plenty of evidence that it can't be. But evolutionists continue to put on their blinders, stop up their blushing ears, and bury their shaking heads in the sand.

Goldschmidt, quoted earlier, tries to get around the lack of evidence by saying, "Evolution of the animal and plant world is considered by *all those entitled to judgment* to be a fact for which no further proof is needed" (*American Scientist*, v. 40, p. 84). Goldschmidt's definition of those entitled to judgment must be confined to those who say, "Please don't confuse me with the facts. My mind is made up."

Julian Huxley, biologist, first Director-General of UNESCO, proclaimed, at the Darwin Centennial Celebration, "No serious scientist would deny that evolution has occurred" (*Evolution after Darwin,* vol. 3, p. 41). His definition of a "serious scientist" is in the same sinking ship with Goldschmidt's definition of "those entitled to judgment."

Evolutionist George Wald, Professor of Biology at Harvard University, makes this profound pronouncement:

"The most complex machine man has ever devised—say an electronic brain—is child's play compared with the simplest of living organisms. . . . One has only to contemplate . . . to concede that the spontaneous generation of a living organism is impossible. Yet here we are—as a result, I believe, of spontaneous generation. . . . Time is in fact the hero of the plot. . . . One has only to wait: time itself performs the miracles" (*The Physics and Chemistry of Life*, p. 9-12, Scientific American, Inc.).

Wald says that one has only to think to know it can't be so, and then he says he believes it anyway. Is that the mark of a true scientist?

Over and over again, evolutionists are found saying that "all true scientists," "all reputable biologists," "most enlightened persons" agree with them, when in fact, the exact opposite is true. "It takes one to know one," is an old adage that might explain what has happened here. A phony scientist, one who ignores the facts that disprove his theory, isn't equipped to recognize the genuine article.

In I Timothy 6:20, Saint Paul warned us against phony scientists. We should have listened when he said:

> O Timothy, keep that which is committed to thy trust, avoiding profane and vain babblings, and oppositions of science falsely so called.*

Smith's article, already quoted in part, raises other interesting questions about the fixity of species, and cites further proof that evolution can't possibly be the answer to how it all began:

---

*The Greek for "science" in this verse is *gnosis*. It refers, most likely, to gnostic religion, a first-century heresy akin to Christian Science. Whenever "science" goes to origins, it goes to gnosticism, because the origin of things is neither repeatable nor observable—therefore, if it is called "science," it is falsely so called.

If present living forms evolved from primitive unicellular forms, why are there still millions of unicellular protozoa in that primitive state living today? Why have they not evolved to a higher state? Also, why are there 15,000 kinds of protozoa living today? If they derived from the first protozoan, why have they remained unicellular and primitive?

Evolutionists date the corals at 500 million years. Why does a close examination of corals show little, if any, change? . . .

The Tuatara is the only one of its reptilian order alive today. Its fossils are dated from the Cretaceous era, but there is no evident difference between the fossils and the living Tuatara, supposedly 135 million years later. The Coelacanth has protuberances with fins on the end. When evolutionists first found fossils of this fish, they said the protuberances were growing legs and that later the fins disappeared. It was claimed the fish had become extinct 300 million years ago. However, some live coelacanth have been caught, and it is noted that the growing legs have not grown and the fins have not disappeared and are still used for swimming.

The capillary tree known as the Gingko or Gingko biloba is dated from the Jurassic era, but after "150 million years" this tree grows in Japan unchanged throughout all these centuries. . . .

Evolution maintains that less complex beings preceded more complex beings. The virus is far less complex than a living cell, but being a parasite, the virus could not live without a hostess cell, and therefore, could not have preceded it. On the other hand, some viruses reproduce every half-hour, making it possible for scientists to observe 17,500 generations within ten years. In all the years of studying the virus, no major mutations have been observed... .

Deoxyribonucleic Acid—DNA

What makes the species, or family, constant? According to scientists, it is the presence of deoxyribonucleic acid in the cell. This DNA is distributed to each of the billions of living cells in your body. It determines the form and the function of each cell. Geneticists have established that the hereditary information of all species is determined by the nitrogenized bases of the DNA molecule. One gene may have as many as 1000 of these units dispensed in such a way as to form a long filament. The genes may align themselves in different ways along the chromosome, making possible the minor differences between people and between animals. One cell may contain tens of thousands of genes, but the particles of DNA carry only hereditary information, so there are no major changes producing new families. The coded instructions contained in just one cell would fill an encyclopedia of 1000 volumes. To believe that all this is produced by chance is . . . absurd. . . .

The substance DNA tolerates no change unless affected by an exterior accident such as irradiation. According to observations of scientists, such changes are not major, but diminutive, not beneficial but harmful, not evolutionary but degrading. . . .

Another important matter for evolutionists and creationists is how to determine the age of fossil remains of once living creatures. Since every living specimen is characterized by carbon compounds (inanimate objects, like rocks for example, do not necessarily contain carbon compounds), carbon testing has been used by evolutionists to date fossils. In the following passage Ray Smith describes and evaluates this method:

The C-14 method . . . was invented by Dr. Libby (1947) who was given the Nobel Prize. Plants get their carbon from the atmosphere, and animals get their carbon from the plants they eat. Most of the carbon in the atmosphere is C-12 which is stable and keeps its identity. C-14 is an isotope of carbon and is less abundant. An isotope . . . emits rays and is radioactive. This radioactivity changes C-14 into nitrogen. In a period of 5730 years, one-half of a

46

given quantity of C-14 is changed into nitrogen. As a living being takes in no more carbon after his death, scientists believe they can calculate the time of its death with a Geiger counter.

There are some things which make this method questionable. We cannot be sure of the amount of C-14 present at the time of the death. We are not sure that the C-14 in the atmosphere was always stable. C-14 is produced by cosmic rays bombarding nitrogen at high altitudes in the atmosphere. These bombardments may be caused by what are commonly called the "Northern Lights" (Aurora borealis) and by the sunspots which sometimes cover as much as one-sixth of the sun's surface. How does this affect the amount of C-14 in the atmosphere? How much C-14 is lost by filtration? Scientists tell us that the magnetic fields of the poles have changed at some time, and this would also affect the amount of C-14 in the atmosphere.

In Siberia frozen mammoths have been found in the ice with tropical vegetation, partly digested, in their stomachs. In Alaska there are great quantities of oil and remains of semi-tropical animals, and in western United States dinosaur remains have been found. It is claimed the largest dinosaurs ate as much as 1000 pounds of food per day. All this indicates that at one time the earth had a universal tropical climate and tropical vegetation. How would this affect C-14? . . .

Having established the uncertainty of Carbon-14 dating, Smith goes on to point out other disadvantages of the C-14 method for the evolutionists' theories:

In a giant international enterprise in which over 90 universities and museums collaborated, more than 15,000 remains of what were once living beings were dated by the revised method of C-14. The results were published in the annual magazine *Radiocarbon*. Here are some results: one Neanderthal man 32,000 years and another 40,000 years. Coal formerly dated at 200 to 300 million years dated at

1680 years. Rhodesian man or "Broken Hill" man dated at 9000 years and bones of Thamesville and Catham, Ontario, dated at 8900 years. Mammiferous bones found at the same site where Dr. Leakey found his "hominid skull" which he claimed was at least 600,000 years old, were given an age of 10,000 years. Bones from the Omo Valley of Ethiopia which were said to have been older than those found by Dr. Leakey were given an age of only 15,000 years. Notice nothing is dated at more than 40,000 years.

By evolutionists' standards 40,000 years is but a passing moment in time. We have already seen that, by their own admission, their theory requires an earth that is millions, if not billions, of years old. Certainly the results of Carbon-14 dating do not offer them much support.

Edsel Murphy Egghead Analog Circular Reasoning—A device used by evolutionists to impress one another and to mislead everybody else. E.g.,

Q.: "How old is this fossil?"
A.: "At least a billion years old."
Q.: "How do you know?"
A.: "Because it was found in a strata at least a billion years old."
Q.: "How do you know the strata is that old?"
A.: "Because it contained a fossil at least a billion years old."

Another question people sometimes ask has to do with improvement within a species. This can look like evolution, but isn't. The cow, for instance, is always a cow—big cow, little cow, fat cow, skinny cow. And you can breed for big horns, you can breed for beef, or you can breed for big brown eyes or milk, but you have not evolved a new species. You have merely improved a given species. Improvement within the species is unlimited, but there's never a crossing over to half cow and half horse or whatever. The species is firmly established by its own extremely complicated genetic coding.

God programmed everything so that it would bring forth after its own kind.* And He hasn't changed His computer.

Has your question been covered? If it hasn't, you might like to subscribe to the *Bible-Science Newsletter,* issued ten times a year by the Bible-Science Association, Inc., Box 1016, Caldwell, Idaho, 83605. Every issue is packed with scientific *facts* confirming the accuracy and validity of the *Manufacturer's Handbook.*

---

*Horses and donkeys can be cross-bred, but the resulting mule is sterile.

Chapter 4

Man Blows It

Adam had it made. He was created in the very image of God by God Himself and placed in the Garden of Eden—perfect plan, perfect workmanship, perfect environment. He even had a perfect wife, tailor-made to suit him exactly. God formed her from one of Adam's ribs, which He took from Adam's body one day while Adam was sleeping. When he woke up and saw her, Adam must have thought he was dreaming. But he wasn't. She was real!

"Eve," he sighed, "you're the only woman in the world for me!"

Now, Adam could have eaten of the tree of life and he would have lived forever. Life in a beautiful garden, no parking problems, a luscious wife, no competition, plenty to eat, no income taxes, no laundry bills, no rowdy neighbors or PTA meetings. Why, he even had fellowship with *God* on a first-hand, personal basis. The Bible says that

51

Adam and God walked together in the cool of the evening. That's close fellowship. Nothing in between them—no shadows, no coverups, no Watergates, no guilt, no sin. Just perfect innocence and freedom.

Can you imagine goofing an idyllic situation like that? Well Adam did, but good.

God had told Adam he could eat of the fruit of every tree in the garden except one, the tree of the knowledge of good and evil. That one was off limits. If he ate of it, God said, he would surely die. If he didn't eat of it, all systems would be go forever.

Before he even got as far as the tree of life, Adam rebelled. He just had to sample that forbidden fruit of the tree of the knowledge of good and evil. Satan, the snake, told Adam's wife, Eve, that if she would eat of that tree, she would be as God, knowing good and evil, and that naturally whetted her appetite. (Up to then, there had been no evil. It was nonexistent. God had pronounced His creation to be very good.)

Her curiosity aroused, Eve didn't resist temptation, she succumbed to it. She ate of the forbidden fruit, and she gave Adam a bite, too.

It'll happen every time. A no-no just naturally creates an appetite in us. If you don't believe it, put a kid in a room with a basketful of beautiful apples and one little old wormy apple. Tell the kid he can eat the whole basket of good apples if he wants to, but that he's not to touch the wormy apple. Then go out of the room for five minutes. When you come back, the beautiful fruit will be there, untouched. And there will be just half a worm inside the wormy apple. The other half will be in the kid. That's our nature.

Adam and Eve ate the forbidden fruit because they wanted to be as God.

God said, "If you eat it, it'll kill you," but what God said was beside the point.

A snake said, "Oh, come now. Surely you don't think God would kill off His favorite creation—mankind? Of course not." His voice was smooth as oil, *so* persuasive. And Adam and Eve weren't wary. They didn't know yet that whenever you begin to reason together, looking to your head for answers instead of to God, you're headed for big trouble. You've had it.

The devil is always a deceitful operator. In real life, he doesn't wear his costume like he does in melodramas. In real life, he never comes on strong in long red underwear and a forked tail, twirling a black moustache. He comes softly, as a smoothie, an angel of light, a beautiful serpent, whatever his disguise might be. And he always begins by casting doubt on the truth and trustworthiness of the Word of God. He always wants to dilute it, to water it down with reasonableness.

Why does the human mind listen to snake talk in preference to God talk? Because, according to Isaiah 1:5, the whole head is sick. Did you think half of your head was dependable? Think again. Not a hair on it, nor anything under the hair, is reliable. It isn't now, it wasn't then. Actually, about the only useful function the head performs—until your mind is regenerated and reprogrammed by God's Holy Spirit—is to keep your ears from flapping together. Our carnal minds have to be renewed and renewed and renewed until we have the very mind of Christ in us. Until that takes place, the less you rely on your mind, the better off you'll be.

Our minds were blown in the Garden of Eden. You don't have to take acid to blow your mind. A blown mind is standard equipment when you're born.

Our minds were blown in the Garden of Eden.

Man's first sin was to trust his own mind instead of trusting the God who made it. The King James translation of the *Manufacturer's Handbook* didn't come out until 1611, and so Adam hadn't read Proverbs 3:5-6 where it says "Lean not to thine own understanding. In all thy ways acknowledge him, and he shall direct thy paths." But it wasn't ignorance of God's will that tripped Adam, it was willfulness, wanting to do his own thing. And he did it.

Immediately, death and decay were set in motion for all his posterity, including us. Adam's first child was a murderer. God cursed the ground, and said, "You'll have to contend with it unless you want to starve to death." Right away, there began to be mutations in the plant kingdom.

Both chemicals and nuclear radiation can cause mutations, which are tortured reprogrammings of the cells of a plant or an animal. We automatically receive some nuclear radiation. When solar rays come from the sun and hit our outer atmosphere, they break down into scatter radiation which we call neutrons. In about thirteen minutes, these neutrons break down into protons and electrons—unless they combine with some other group to make an element. In the process, they are emitting radiation, causing life to diminish, to be destroyed.

You can take a radish seed, which is smooth and regular and produces a well-organized leaf and plant, and expose it to nuclear radiation. Afterward, you can plant it, and what will come up? The ugliest, thorniest, thistle you ever saw. If you know somebody who has a nuclear reactor, who will let you take your seeds and put them in it before you plant them, you can raise a garden full of hideous mutants.

That there were mutations in the plant kingdom after Adam's fall is clear from Genesis 3:17-18 which says, "And to Adam, God said, 'Because you listened to your wife and ate the fruit when I told you not to, I have placed a curse upon the soil. All your life you will struggle to extract a living from it. It will grow thorns and thistles for you' " (TLB). Adam hadn't seen any thorns and thistles before he sinned. There weren't any then. But we've had a more than adequate supply of them ever since.

Not only did the plant kingdom take a turn for the worse when Adam sinned, but the animal kingdom became enemies of people. Everything took a nose dive because of original sin, which is another name for Adam's goof.

Not long after Adam came down with original sin, everybody else caught it, and things got so bad that God was sorry He had made man in the first place. Why, man was so wicked, the Bible says, that the thoughts of his heart were only evil continually. And God made up His mind He'd have to start the whole thing over again from scratch, because the old mess wasn't worth patching up.

But there was still one man who had stayed in touch with Him, and so God gave that man an assignment.

"Noah," He said, "it's going to rain. And there's going to be a flood. I want you to build an ark." He gave him very specific directions, better than a blueprint, about what he should make it from, and just what the dimensions were to be. "This will be the ark of deliverance," He said. "Whoever goes aboard will be saved; whoever doesn't will drown." There was no in between, no second chance.

This was heavy stuff for Noah, because there were no words in his vocabulary for rain or flood. The weather had been perfect up to then, and everything got watered by a mist that rose up from the ground (Gen. 2:6). They hadn't even invented umbrellas yet. Noah certainly didn't need a boat on dry land, and he didn't know what God was talking about. But he figured God did, and that was good enough for him. He started to work.

Can't you imagine what the neighbors thought when they heard him hammering and came over to stand on the sidewalk and superintend the job?

"Brother Noah, what's that big old thing parked out in your driveway?"

"That's an ark."

"An ark? What's that?"

"Well, it's a kind of a boat—like a floodmobile—for safety from the flood."

"The flood? What's that?"

"I don't know, exactly, but God said He was going to send one. It'll be made out of rain."

"Rain? What's that?"

They were dealing in absolute unknowns, but Noah knew God and trusted Him. And when it came time to go aboard the ark, the animals didn't argue. The unclean animals came two by two and the clean ones came seven by seven and marched up the gangplank, waving goodbye to their relatives who stayed behind. But the human race was too intelligent to join the parade. They used their common sense.

"You mean this kooky old preacher Noah thinks he knows more than Professor Tinkling Cymbal down at our Sanhedrinite Theological Cemetery? Why, he and Dr. Sounding Brass have just co-authored a paper in which they prove that God couldn't possibly destroy His favorite creation."

"Forget it, brother. Everybody knows that Noah's an old kook."

Can you imagine how they ridiculed Noah? A man listening to God is always out of step with the world. He doesn't mind it, but the world usually does.

"There you have it, folks, the lighter side of the six o'clock news: Mr. Noah and his floodmobile!"

58

And so they backed off, they stayed away in droves. Only eight people ended up in the ark with all the animals. Noah, his wife, their three sons and their wives. Only eight people out of the whole human race were stupid enough to listen to God in the face of all the learned evidence to the contrary. Those eight were saved. The rest gurgled under the flood and were seen no more, except as fossils.

When the waters receded, the human population of the world was eight people, all saved from the flood by God's special provision. But instead of keeping the world all newly washed and clean, man turned to his own ways again, and became more evil than ever. Even Noah got drunk. God sent fire and brimstone on Sodom and Gomorrah, and the only reason He didn't wipe out all of creation again with another flood was that He kept seeing rainbows—and they reminded Him of His promise to Noah that He'd never send another flood to destroy the world.

In the beginning, man didn't look like a hairless ape—he looked like God. And he didn't act like a hairless ape—until he decided to disobey God and eat of the forbidden fruit. Disobedience and rebellion made a monkey out of him, and from that day, he began to deteriorate from the glory in which God had created him. The "facts" of evolution are just backward from what really happened.

The first man, instead of being a mutant, a freak ape who would have died out in a couple of generations, was so full of life he hung around the earth for nine hundred thirty years—even though he ate a deadly poison when he was still a young man. But from then until now, the natural lifespan of man has diminished.

In the very beginning, the vapor barrier around the world filtered out the nuclear radiation from the sun. But when God let the vapor barrier fall as part of the water that flooded the earth, the filter was broken, and the radiation reaching us increased. And as the nuclear radiation increased, our lifespan diminished. Things went from good to bad and from bad to worse because man made the wrong choice.

But there's no need for us to blame Adam for all that ails us. Given a choice between obedience to God and doing his own thing, man would still choose the wrong way. We are still capable of goofing it—that talent has never left us.

Without God, every atom in all creation has been in torment ever since God put a curse on His creation. Nothing is settled in itself, nothing is satisfied with anything outside itself—until Jesus comes to give peace.

Is this some nonsensical religious notion? No, it is an established fact.

The law of repulsion is built right into the core of every atom in existence. Any physicist—pagan or believer in God—will tell you that the core of the atom is totally disturbed, unhappy, striving to grab onto something to obtain completeness—or to give up something in order to be a whole something instead of one plus an extra piece of leftover tagging along. The scientists even have a name for it—Coulomb's law of mutual repulsion.

What holds atoms together then? Why don't we have atomic blasts going on all the time without our having to go to a lot of trouble to unglue the atom to release the explosive energy that's inside?

That's an interesting question.

If you ask a pagan scientist, "What holds atoms together?" he'll clear his throat and say, "Well, er, ah—there's a force that holds atoms together. We call it 'binding power.' "

If you ask him what the binding power is, he'll look at

his digital computer wristwatch and tell you he's sorry, but he's about to be late for another appointment.

No pagan scientist can tell you what this essential binding power is that keeps atoms from blowing up in our faces continually.

But the apostle Paul knew what it was—because God had told him all about it. When he was writing to the church at Colossae, he told them that Jesus is the visible representation of the invisible God, that in Him all things were created, that all things exist through Him and in and for Him, and that "in Him all things consist—cohere, *are held together*" (Col. 1:17 TAB, italics mine).

In Him you are complete. Without Him, you are programmed for repulsion.

The nuclei of your atoms contain an assortment of miserable particles, protons and neutrons clustered into a group. They hate one another. They repel one another. They're trying their best to blow up, to get away from one another.

In physics, it's called randomness. The atoms in a piece of metal that look solid are in a state of torment wandering around in that metallic structure in random fashion, seeking for completeness, seeking to take on something or to give up something. That's due to the curse that God placed on the whole creation when His chosen people, mankind, chose to disobey God and do their own thing. That's how deeply original sin reads out in every one of your atoms. The nucleus of every one of your atoms is in the same state of torment or randomness.

We cannot overcome it in physics. We can't overcome it in metallurgy. An airplane wing drops right off without any warning. A bridge collapses suddenly, because the atoms cannot tolerate one another, and they go into what's called a "slip plane" within the crystal structure. We make bridges stronger than they need to be to compensate for this possibility, and we do all sorts of things to metal to try to overcome this inherent defect. We call it stress relieving.

But the human personality is never stress-relieved until Jesus moves in and brings peace into the center of every atom of our being. He's the only one who can bring us into the solid state, where all parts work together in harmony toward a common goal. Without Him, we're in an amorphous state, like window glass, ready to shatter into a million pieces if someone fails to handle us with kid gloves.

Edsel Murphy Egghead Analog Solid State—Mistaking a tubful of fast-setting epoxy cement for bubblebath.

Talk about touchy! That's us—without Jesus.

The wages of sin—what we get into when we fall short of the best God has planned for us—is death. Every man has inherited the fruit of Adam's rebellion, and death is still its consequence. Men die. As a matter of fact, they are born dead, and remain in corpsehood all their lives unless they are born again of the Spirit of God. Then they will live forever, enjoying eternal life.

You can never rest quietly until you know Jesus. You've got to have all kinds of things going on. Entertainment—a boob tube for each eyeball. Noise—walk down the street with a blasting transistor radio for each ear. Something to do with your mouth, something to do with your hands. No balance, no equilibrium. No nothing—

except misery—until you enter God's rest, the rest promised to those who believe in Him, who trust Him, who come to Him. (Hebrews 4 or Matthew 11:28, take your pick.)

In God's rest, all forces are balanced out; there is no struggle. Jesus says, "Be perfect." That means, "Be complete, be whole," and there's no way to do it without Him. He is the Rock, and He makes us *solid*.

"Mine iniquities are gone over my head," David said when he was overwhelmed by fear, anxiety, worry. It was the same way with me before I met Jesus. On those rare oc-

---

Edsel Murphy Egghead Analog Orbital Mechanics—Psychiatrists without Jesus. They go around in circles.

---

casions when I had nothing to worry about, I worried about that. It was too good to last. Something bad was bound to happen.

I couldn't enjoy the relatively good times for worrying about what would happen when they were taken away. No question about it, I wasn't much better off than a dead man. In fact, I *was* a dead man. But I wasn't alone. I had lots of company. Almost everybody around me was dead, too.

Death doesn't take away physical life. Death is what is left over after life has departed. A century ago, man's life expectancy was only about thirty years. Today, we've boosted it to seventy, keeping the corpses quivering forty years longer by cramming all kinds of chemicals into their veins. But chemically induced quivering is a long way off from born-again vitality. Pills, ointments, and tranquilizers can't touch real life.

Compare our seventy years—with additives—with the nine-hundred-and-some years Adam stuck around after he took poison into his system. His spiritual death took place when he took the first bite of the forbidden fruit. But it took all those centuries for the enormous vitality that God placed in the human race in the beginning to die out of his physical body. Today, we've reached the point where we can't build nursing homes fast enough to accommodate the corpses who are still breathing.

Chapter 5

Can Man Be Recycled?

The condition of fallen man looks pretty hopeless, doesn't it? The apostle Paul cried out, "O wretched man that I am! Who shall deliver me from this body of death?" Sometimes it looks as if we'll just keep on going down the sliding board until there's nothing left of us except our blisters. Then they'll burst, and we'll be gone. Annihilated.

In the natural, that's what would happen to us, all right, according to the second law of thermodynamics. But because God understood how it would go unless He intervened, He built a remedy for sin and death right into the system. He made a way for us to live, after all, not just to hang around for thirty years or seventy years, or even for nine hundred and thirty years. He made a way for us to live forever, just as we could have done if Adam and Eve hadn't taken things into their own hands and applied their own rotten reasonableness to what God had said.

The way to live forever doesn't begin with patching up what we are now with chemical additives or crutches or the like. The way to eternal life begins with a new beginning. We have to start over, to be born again. We have to die to ourselves in a flood of water baptism and rise to newness of life.

Hillism:
Under His wings, fetters become feathers.

This second birth is not a physical rebirth but a spiritual one. And it happens when we trust Jesus to save us from all that we are and all that Adam was. Dying on the cross, Jesus paid the penalty for all our turning away from God and made us holy in His sight.

And how do we get this gift that God provided through Jesus because He loved us too much to let us perish in our own way? Simply by accepting it.

How do I know? It happened to me.

I tried life my own way for forty-eight years, and I didn't like the outcome. I was a successful, but tormented, empty, miserable, striving, struggling, dreary, drab corpse trying to live it up. What a drag! A graveyard dweller trying to do his thing in a cemetery full of dead things. The law of sin and death had set in for me—but good.

I met Jesus shortly thereafter, and now, crowding seventy, I'm closer to thirty than I was at twenty-nine, because I'm hooked up with the Head Man of the universe, the One who made it all in the first place. I have in me the vital energy of God that He intended from the beginning to be the life of His people. But we blew it when we took our own way of darkness, worshiping our Educated Idiot Box, that calcium deposit on the top eight inches of our skeleton, instead of worshiping God and following His way of light.

Jesus' blood is the antidote for the deadly poison of our rebellion. And it doesn't work by any gradual, evolutionary process. The truth is, we don't need changing, we need wiping out. We need to start all over, be born again, and become new creatures with no hangover from the past. Strangely enough, that's exactly what He promises to do for us when we turn to Him.

"Therefore if any man be in Christ, he is a new creature: old things are passed away; behold, all things are become new" (II Cor. 5:17).

"And you, who were dead in trespasses and the uncircumcision of your flesh, God made alive together with him, having forgiven us all our trespasses" (Col. 2:13 RSV).

From death to life in one fell swoop is a whole lot better than gradual change. Gradually, the dead decompose. Resurrection is all of a sudden. And I'm in favor of resurrection, aren't you?

There's nothing unscientific about resurrection. We see it all the time in nature. A grain of wheat falls into the ground and dies, the winter snow covers it, and then all of a sudden it's spring. The dead grain springs up into a new stalk, and before long, its ears are heavy with new kernels of grain.

How do you go about being resurrected, raised from the dead, born again to start all over as a brand-new creature so alive that you will live forever?

The formula is so simple that the world refuses to believe it. They'd rather stay dead than to do something as simple as following the directions in the *Manufacturer's*

The truth is, we don't need changing, we need wiping out.

Handbook. They're there, plain as day, steps 1-2-3.

In the Book of Romans, Paul wrote, under the inspiration of the Holy Spirit of God: "If you confess with your lips that Jesus is Lord and believe in your heart that God raised him from the dead, you will be saved" (10:9).

Easy enough, isn't it? Just say, "Jesus is my Lord," and believe in your heart that God raised Him from the dead, and you are automatically saved from death. You enter into the new creaturehood of II Corinthians 5:17, and that includes eternal life. The whole works. It's promised in John 3:16:

> For God so loved the world, that he gave his only begotten Son, that whosoever believeth in him should not perish, but have everlasting life.

That sure beats evolving from dead to decomposed.

Hillism:
**Life without Jesus will end
in alcohol, pills, or windowsills.**

Chapter 6

Where Do We Go from Here?

Once we have been resurrected, raised from our own deadness by accepting the brand-new life Jesus came to bring us, then what?

The first thing to realize is that Jesus' gift of new creaturehood is not like gifts the world gives you. They ring your doorbell, make the delivery, and take off, leaving you on your own as far as using the gift is concerned. But Jesus doesn't give you new creaturehood, wave goodbye, and take off. He sticks right there with you, living His life through you. Where the things of God are concerned, the Giver comes with the gift—and stays forever. "I'm the way," He says, "and I'll never leave you or forsake you."

Pretty good bargain, isn't it? A perfect new life with a built-in maintenance man in exchange for an old life that was ready for the graveyard.

And as we learn to yield to His new life in us, things

get better and better. Colossians 2:10 says that you are complete in Him. There's nothing lacking in your life when you're complete in Jesus. If that once gets hold of your gizzard, you'll never have to struggle for anything again. But if it doesn't—if you let doubt and unbelief grip your gizzard instead, you'll fight a losing battle all the way and miss out on the best God has for you. You'll be a billy-goat Christian, always saying, "Yes, but—"

When God had led the children of Israel out of Egypt to the land He had promised them, they could have just walked in and taken it over. No sweat. But they refused to take His word for it that the victory would be theirs. He said He'd make all the arrangements for them, but their gizzards were full of unbelief, full of trusting themselves instead of trusting God.

"We must be very careful, brethren," they said. "We'd better send some spies in and check this thing out. Maybe God doesn't know what He's talking about."

And so they formed a church committee to judge the Word of God, to see whether or not God knew what He was talking about. And that's where the trouble started. A church committee is a good thing when it minds its own business. But when it sets out to snoop into God's business, to see if God is telling the truth or maybe pulling a fast one, that same committee is a dreadful thing. It judges by common sense, and common sense comes from a sick head, so it gets sick answers.

The committee sent spies into the Promised Land. There they saw giants so large they made the spies look—and feel—like grasshoppers. But two of the spies, Joshua and Caleb, saw something that impressed them even more than the giants did. They saw a beautiful land flowing with milk and honey, a land so fertile that it took two men just to carry a single bunch of grapes!

The other spies were more impressed with the giants than with the grapes. But Joshua and Caleb said, "Aw, don't worry about the giants. God promised He'd take care of them for us. We just have to go in and possess the land. That's all. It's already ours because God said so."

But the two who were sold on the truth of God's Word were outvoted by the unbelieving majority who relied on their good common sense instead of on the promises of God.

What happened to the unbelievers? Did they get to enter the Promised Land anyway? No, God let them all drop dead in the wilderness, every single one of them, the whole generation. Because of their unbelief, because they refused to believe what God told them, they perished. Joshua and Caleb were the only ones among them who survived to enter the Promised Land, many years later.

We need to understand something about unbelief so we won't goof our own chances to receive all that God has promised and done for us.

Unbelief is not simply a lack of faith. It is a negative power generated by an act of will in the human head which says, "No, thank You, God. I'll believe the dead doctrines of men instead of trusting in Your living Word. Your way just doesn't sound reasonable to me; it just doesn't make sense. It sounds too supernatural, or something. Besides, my grandpa didn't believe like that, and he was a deacon for forty years, so I won't believe that way either."

In physics, such negative power is known as bias. Bias voltage is very useful for control purposes in an electronic circuit. We can use it as a gate to stop the flow of positive power.

Our human mechanism is an electronic mechanism, a bunch of electromagnetic wave patterns, and so is all the

Unbelief is not simply
a lack of faith. It is an act of will
which says, "No thank you, God."

74

rest of creation as far as we know. At least, everything seems to behave in the way that electromagnetic wave patterns do.

When you, by an act of your will, inject the bias, the negative energy, of unbelief into the human mind, it closes down your receptivity mechanism. You become a blockhead—blocked from God's best by your deliberate, willful negative bias.

In the biochemistry of the human heart, the bias, the negativity, of guilt, unforgiveness, and resentment can effectively paralyze the heart muscle so that it can no longer flex and pump blood. A heart on strike doesn't do the rest of your body a whole lot of good, no matter now healthy it might have seemed to start with.

Christians are given a whole lot of armor—a girdle of truth, a breastplate of righteousness, footwear of the gospel of peace, a shield of faith, a helmet of salvation—and a weapon—the sword of the Spirit (read Ephesians 6)—to protect them from outside attacks by the enemy. But we can still be destroyed from the inside, from the negative bias we *let* settle in our hearts and minds to keep us from living it up in the eternal life Jesus died to give us.

The negativity of unforgiveness, guilt, and resentment can actually throw the heart mechanism out of synchronization. Guilt interferes with the voltages that control the heart action—the negative bias that God puts on it to hold it closed, the positive voltage that causes it to pulse in proper rhythm. A heart subjected to the strains of unforgiveness, guilt, fear, anxiety, and unrest suffers from scatter or random voltages and goes into all sorts of weird off-beat mutational pulsations, palpitations, and murmurings.

Lieutenant Ralph Maxwell is a member of the Baltimore Fire Department Paramedical Unit, a model being studied and followed by other units throughout the country. His outfit, trained in techniques for on-the-spot cardiac treatment for highway accident cases, utilizing radio-consultation with specialists in twenty-two area hospitals, has been responsible for saving many lives. Lieutenant Maxwell wrote me:

> For the past several years, I have been responsible for training paramedical personnel to deliver Advanced Emergency Cardiac Care for the Baltimore Metropolitan Region. During this time, I have noted a definite connection between hardening of the spiritual heart and hardening of the arteries within the physical body.
>
> While there are several reasons for a person becoming a high-risk candidate for a heart attack, one in particular has interested me. Studies indicate that when a person lives under fear, worry, and stress, the body produces a higher than normal level of the hormone adrenalin within the bloodstream. When the adrenalin level within the body is excessive for prolonged periods of time, it pulls substances from the fatty tissues and produces a cholesterol buildup at an accelerated rate on the arterial walls, resulting in arteriosclerosis or hardening of the arteries.
>
> For the heart muscle to contract, it must be stimulated by an electrical impulse that originates near the top of the heart and spreads throughout the heart muscle, causing contraction. Hardening of the arteries causes irritability of the heart muscle which in turn can become a real threat to life itself.
>
> Several years ago, I placed a monitor on a heart patient to record his heart activity. He was instructed to keep a log of his activities and return for examination after eight hours. Later, while evaluating his EKG, I found his heart had produced a potentially life-threatening rhythm while he was watching a world news report on national television.
>
> The Bible says in Luke 21:26, "Men's hearts failing them for fear and for looking after those things which are coming on the earth." The Book of Hebrews (3:7-8) says, "Today, if you will hear His voice, harden not your hearts."

How does one harden his spiritual heart toward God? By permitting the things of this world and all its concerns and interests to pass through his heart without restriction. Then the heart loses its tenderness toward God and becomes hardened, spiritually as well as physically. But when the Word of God is received into the spiritual heart by much meditation on His Word, the physical heart is kept by the Spirit which produces peace, joy, and love which are conducive to good health. When the Word of God is shared with someone who refuses to receive it and act upon it, that person actually hardens his heart toward God, with detrimental results.

Even non-spiritual, unconverted cardiologists have documented proof that a person's chances of heart attack are greatly increased when he or she is engaged in sexual activity with someone else's husband or wife. Practicing what is known to be against God's Word can produce not only hardening of the arteries, and heart attack, but many other illnesses within the body.

"My heart panteth," the psalmist said. That's the best word the Bible translators could think of to describe heart trouble from the bad things we let settle in our gizzards. And modern technology documents it—that when a man's heart is not right toward God and his fellowman, trouble is building up inside. But if we follow the plain instructions in the *Manufacturer's Handbook,* we'll be so forgiving of others, we'll confess our sins so regularly, that unforgiveness and guilt won't be in us. Our hearts will be free from the ravages of sin.

Heart trouble isn't the only ailment we can expect to have if we ignore the instructions God has given us for abundant life. Many painful cases of arthritis are known to have their origin in resentment. You turn a cold shoulder to someone, and your body can't stand the reduced temperature. Coldness causes calcium to settle in the joint. Arthritis sets in. Pretty soon, you can't raise your arm to wave hello—even to someone you like.

Every instruction in the *Manufacturer's Handbook* is there that we might enjoy abundant life with Him forever—no aches, no pains, no frustration—all righteousness, peace, and joy. That's what His Kingdom is made of.

Jesus summed up all the rules for us when He said, "Love God with all your heart and soul and mind—and love your neighbor as yourself."

"Oh," you say, "that sounds good, but I can never do it. Why, I can hardly even stand myself some days, let alone love anybody else."

Good! That's where the next step of the program comes in. God has made such excellent provision for your new creaturehood that He sends His own Holy Spirit to live in you, to give you power to live the kind of life you want to live now that you have been born again and have power to become a son of God. And all you have to do to get this Holy Spirit is to ask for it!

Chapter 7

You and the Holy Spirit

Time now to back up and review what we've said so far before we proceed with the rest of it.

In the beginning, God created. The evolutionist says that in the beginning, a little simple cell appeared and wriggled in a primordial swamp, and after millions of years, it evolved into the human race of hairless apes. But the second law of thermodynamics, the second law of science based on observable fact, says that there has never been an interchange of energy that did not come under the law of increasing disorder.

The Bible calls it the law of sin and death. You're stuck with degeneration, deterioration. From the day you're born, you begin to die.

Given enough time, says the evolutionist, we will evolve into something gloriously wonderful. Given enough time, says the second law of physics, we will decay, degenerate, and fall apart. Heat never becomes hotter. The hot becomes the cold; the light becomes the dark; the living becomes the dead. And in a few hundred years, the organized becomes the disorganized. The simple never becomes the complex over a period of time, the theories of the evolutionists notwithstanding.

In an act of creation, God made man to have dominion over the rest of His creation. Our original parents blew that arrangement, but God reinstated it in Jesus. And now, having been born again, of the Spirit, by trusting Jesus, we know that living in the soul (mind and emotion) is death. All we had to live in, prior to our rebirth, was soul and body. We were two-dimensional, empty, dreary, drab corpses without Jesus. We had length and width, but no depth at all. Before Jesus, we were shallow people. There is no depth or capacity for God in a two-dimensional corpse.

But when we have received Jesus, we are alive in God because we have been born again in Jesus Christ. And Jesus in us is the Light of the world.

The Bible says we have this treasure—this priceless treasure, Jesus—in earthen vessels (II Corinthians 4:7). We are the vessels, He is the treasure. Once upon a time I had sort of looked at it this way—that if you could cut me open and look within, you'd find Jesus down inside there in a little velvet-lined compartment. But one day recently, I saw that Jesus actually suffuses every atom of our beings. He's not down inside in just one little pocket. If you could slice open every single atom of your body, you'd find Jesus in the nucleus of every one. Without Him there, you'd find total torment. You would see more empty space than anything else, because according to the classical diagram, an atom consists of orbiting shells of electrons spaced far apart from each other. Scientists have said that the total effect is about like standing out in the open on a starry night and looking into the heavens. The distance between you and the farthest star represents the empty space between the nucleus of an atom and the outer electron shell. Vast emptiness surrounds the nucleus—until Jesus comes in to fill all things according to His promise in Ephesians 1:23. Before that happens, before your regeneration, every atom of your being is trying to explode, to blow up. One of the greatest mysteries among secular scientists, scientists without knowledge of God, is "Why doesn't the atom explode the instant it's formed because of this tremendous explosive energy built in?"

The Bible is the only textbook I own that explains that Jesus is the binding power that holds the atom together.

You're an explosive bomb, a mixture of turmoil and misery, until Jesus moves in. This accounts for the fact that human beings are so often repulsive to one another. The law of mutual repulsion is built into every atom, and into everyone of us. Coulomb's law of mutual repulsion says that likes always repel.

After we're born-again, the repelling principle is reversed, and Jesus draws us together. Every man-made fellowship has a tendency to fall apart. We try to glue them together with circuses and bake sales and clam bakes and hoe-downs and fix-ups and all kinds of make-work things. But when we become born-again and Spirit-filled, you can't keep us apart. Jesus holds us together in proper order and union. Colossians 2 tells us that we are also completed in Him. Our orbits are filled out, satisfied, by Jesus and only by Him.

Being born-again is not just a subjective experience, it's a demonstrable scientific fact. There is acually a scientific instrument that can detect whether or not you are born-again, whether or not you have the Light of the world in you. A friend of mine, Dr. Donald Liebman, has developed what I call a glory meter.

Dr. Liebman is a "completed Jew," one who has met Jesus as his Messiah—his Savior and Baptizer in the Holy Spirit. The laboratory instrument he developed is used in brain research to measure the energy within the human mechanism. It can calibrate the light, the energy level, within your structure prior to your rebirth, after your rebirth, and after you have been baptized with the Holy Spirit. There are remarkable differences!

When you're born into this world, the light that lighteth every man coming into this world (John 1:9) measures between eight and ten on the scale, way down on the bottom end. It's just enough to get you moving, to start you off, a booster shot that lasts long enough to get you born again. But if you're stupid enough or stubborn enough to avoid or evade that second birth, you'll soon find out that the booster shot wasn't designed to get you very far down the road of life. You'll begin to peter out in your seventh year, and by the time you're forty, you'll be living on chemical additives to keep the corpse quivering. Pagans live their lives in that land of darkness, close by the gates of death, just barely alive, and Dr. Liebman's instrument can detect it.

When you say yes to Jesus, and He moves in, not as an intellectual idea in your head, but as a living reality in your heart, down where you live, the meter reading goes up between fifty and sixty, above the middle of the dial. You're born again, a new creature, a baby Christian, really alive. According to John 1:12, when you received Him, He gave you the power—the energy—to become a son of God.

Jesus didn't present the born-again experience as an option. He said it was an absolute necessity. 'Ye *must* be born again" (John 3:7). The born-again experience is not just a good thing. It's not to make you good. It's to make you alive! You're just plain dead without it.

But that's not all. There's another step—the Baptism in the Holy Spirit. Before we have that, we are half-scale Christians, half-baked, half-power, like an automobile with half the cylinders taken out of the engine. Oh, you'll clunk along, but you won't have a smooth ride, and you won't really get anywhere or be able to help anyone else much along the way.

In John 1:29, 33 we read, "Behold the Lamb of God, which taketh away the sin of the world . . . the same is he which baptizeth with the Holy Ghost." Luke 3:16 says, "He shall baptize you with the Holy Ghost and with fire." Matthew and Mark say much the same thing. Jesus saves us, and Jesus baptizes us, two distinct and separate functions which sometimes occur simultaneously, depending on how far you sold out to Jesus in the beginning.

As our living Savior, Jesus Christ comes into us through a personal encounter. He energizes our body, brings us to life, and then He says, "I'd like to baptize you in My Holy Spirit. I'd like to give you power, and energize you to be My witness."

The reading on Dr. Liebman's meter zooms up over a hundred, to the top of the scale when it's hooked up to a born-again, Spirit-baptized Christian. Liebman's going to have to make the scale longer, because it's too short to measure the total energy in that kind of lit-up Christian. The word *Christian* really means "little anointed one." Isn't it something that an objective scientific instrument can recognize the anointing!

For clarification: Every Christian is baptized *by* the Holy Spirit *into* the body of Christ when we're born again (I Cor. 12:13). That's the baptism *of* the Holy Spirit. The baptism of (by) Jesus *in* (or *with*) the Holy Spirit takes place when we go to Jesus for the second transaction (Luke 3:16). When that happens, when the Holy Ghost comes upon us (Acts 1:8), we receive power—and we become His witnesses.

When we receive the Holy Spirit in His fullness, we don't have to *choose* to be witnesses; it's an automatic thing. Jesus said, "Ye *shall* be witnesses unto me." No ifs or buts about it. A witness is somebody who sees something, and the Holy Spirit opens our eyes to who God is and what He's doing. Whether your natural vision is 20/20 or you need a seeing-eye dog, when you are baptized in the Holy Spirit, you'll be like Peter and John when they said, "We cannot but speak of the things which we have seen and heard" (Acts 3:20), because the Holy Spirit opens your eyes and reveals God to you (Eph. 1:17-19 TEV).

You think maybe the Holy Spirit is not for you? When Peter stood up to preach on the day of Pentecost, he quoted the prophet Joel who quoted God as saying, "I will pour out of My spirit on *all* flesh." That "all flesh" probably includes you, unless you're made of plastic or some other synthetic. And when his congregation asked him what they could do to get right with God, Peter told them to repent, to be baptized, and they would "receive the gift of the Holy Ghost. For the promise is unto you, and to your children, and to all that are afar off, even as many as the Lord our God shall call" (Acts 2:38-39). Sounds like that could include you, too, doesn't it?

Sometimes people try to weasel out of qualifying for a top score on Liebman's glory meter by saying, "I'm too much for God to handle."

Forget it. All have sinned and come short of the glory of God. You've no right to think you're that much worse than the rest of us. And really, when you consider it, a corpse is

You're an explosive bomb, a mixture of turmoil and misery until Jesus moves in.

not too hard to handle anyhow. It doesn't have much resistance left in it. All you have to do is give up. Abandon all your do-it-yourself schemes. Ask Jesus to take over, and stop trying to understand what's going to happen. Then, watch it happen. New creaturehood—not while you wait—but ZAP, just like that, in the twinkling of an eye, at the speed of light. Not because you're worthy—but because God loves you!

In one of John's letters, he sums it up for us:

> See what an incredible quality of love the Father has given us, that we should be the children of God! and so we are! Beloved, we are now God's children; it is not yet disclosed what we shall be hereafter, but we know that when He comes, we shall be like Him, for we shall see Him just as He really is (I John 3:1-2 TAB).

That's not evolution; that's being changed from glory to glory as we look at Him, the One who created us in His image.

What a future is in store for us who believe in Him! And we are called to be King's kids in the here and now.

In the fullness of the Spirit of God, all frustration is gone. Everything is in equilibrium and at rest. All forces are balanced. This is the power of the Holy Spirit. As you approach the speed of light, things slow down. At the speed of light, things stand still, and beyond the speed of light, some scientists speculate that things might run backward. We don't know for sure, because we haven't gone that fast yet.

God is light. In God, there is no change. The laws of physics and the laws of science and the Bible fit together perfectly because our God is the overall designer. You don't have to show the ravages of time if you're resting in the rest that remains for the people of God.

Time is reversible up and down the scale at the point of light where God is. He can run backward or forward, because at the speed of light, there is the timelessness of eternity. God spoke about it long ago when He said, "Before they call, I will answer. And while you're yet speaking will I hear, if you're walking in the light" (Isa. 65:24 AP). We're discovering things every day in the world of science that God put in His Book thousands of years ago. (See the Appendix II for some of them.)

The first verse of chapter nine of the Book of Revelation has been mysterious to us until very recently: "And the fifth angel sounded, and I saw a star fall from heaven unto the earth, and to him was given the key to the bottomless pit." Not long ago, astronomers discovered something like a bottomless pit, up in the north sky.

Radio waves aimed in that direction are absorbed. Light beams are absorbed. Everything that goes into that pit is swallowed up; it disappears completely—without a trace, into a big black hole. It sounds like the bottomless pit referred to in Revelation.

Scientists theorize that there might have been a tremendous heavenly body—at least three times the size of our sun—that suddenly collapsed, leaving a tremendous force of gravity without mass. Such a gravitational force would draw into itself every thing it could suck in, just like a powerful vacuum cleaner, the garbage disposal system of the universe. Someday Satan is going to be tossed into a bottomless pit, a black hole (Rev. 20:1-3).

It sounds scary, and these days, pagans *are* running scared. But King's kids are not going to have to deal with those things. I'm interested in light, the very reverse of darkness. The Scripture says God is light, and in Him is no darkness at all. Darkness is actually the lack of anything, the absence of energy, the absence of light. Light is energy. Light is real. It behaves like matter. And when we are centered in Jesus, when we are walking in the Spirit, when we are in contact with God, we are within a circle of light, protected from the enemy. Satan can't put a finger on King's kids; he can't talk them into eating any bad apples. It is vitally important to stay in the light.

At the speed of light, life processes stand still. God says, "I am the eternal one. I change not. I am that I am."

We discovered something interesting about timelessness when we sent the astronauts into outer space. When the Apollo astronauts came back from their thirteenth mission, they reportedly calculated the amount of money that they should refund to the government because they spent less time on their round trip than we spent on the earth waiting for them.

The faster you go, the less time it takes to make a trip. If we can send a space vehicle at a hundred and eighty thousand miles per second out into space, we can visit a galaxy fifty trillion miles away and come back in a round trip of seventy years. While the astronauts are traveling the total elapsed time of seventy years, the earth will age three million years. At the speed of light, there is no aging at all.

We're bringing in intelligent radio signals from outer space continually by way of radio telescopes, and we are recording them.* We can't translate them as yet, but one of these days, we hope to acquire at least a little bit of knowledge compared to the folks who are sending the signals. When we are able to decode them, we may find the people

---

*Heard on BBC shortwave broadcast direct from Jodrell Bank Observatory in England, reporting their huge radio-telescope reception of "intelligent radio messages incapable of being deciphered at our present state of intelligence."

from outer space on some other planet saying, "Earth people, why don't you get with it? Why do you stay so stupid? Why don't you ask Jesus to become your wisdom, your righteousness, your sanctification, and redemption? (See I Corinthians 1:30.) You have cooked up a system of theology and religion which has a form of godliness but denies the power thereof. Why don't you get with it? Why don't you turn on to Jesus?"

Indeed, it *is* time for us all to get with it—to become Jesus-centered persons, ready for His return. If you read carefully the biblical prophecies about the things that must happen before the second coming of Jesus, you can know that most of them have been fulfilled. The fact that He is coming again is as reliable as the fact that He came in the first place. It is time for each man to choose between the one who will be thrown into the blackness of the bottomless pit and the One who will rule forever and ever in the kingdom of light.

You can settle all doubts about *your* future—right now. Your place in the "good place" with Jesus forever will be reserved for you as you pray this prayer:

Lord Jesus Christ, please come into my heart right now and save me. Wash away all that filthiness, guilt, and fear down inside where I live. Purify me with Your shed blood and wash me whiter than snow. Make me a completely new person and fill that awful, empty, God-shaped hole with Yourself. Come and live inside me. Live Your life through me, beginning now and continuing forever.

Thank You for Your beautiful peace and assurance that my record is gone, that I'm right with God, and that from now on, I can look to You, knowing that You are in charge of my life and affairs. Change me to suit Yourself. Help Yourself to me completely. And if I'm not sincere in all this—please just go ahead and do it *anyhow*. Thank You, Jesus. Amen.

King's kid, you have just claimed your inheritance as a son of God! Sign your name and date on the dotted line below, recording for history that today you became a King's kid. Get your friends to turn in their raunchy lives for brand-new ones, too, and sign their names along with yours. Then write me a note to let me in on the Good News of the brand-new additions to the Kingdom of the King. Address Harold Hill, King's Kid, c/o Logos, Plainfield, N.J. 07061.

Name .... Date ....

Name .... Date ....

Name .... Date ....

Name .... Date ....

Learn more about *How to Live Like a King's Kid* by reading the book with that title (Plainfield, N.J.: Logos, 1974).

Appendix I

Things Apes Never Do
or
How Human Behavior Differs From that of Other Creatures

The Bible (Genesis 1:26-27) says that God made man in His own image and that He gave him dominion over all the other creatures. If that is true we ought to be able to observe it. In fact, the behavioral scientist, Adler, has already observed it for us and nicely cataloged his findings. They were published in the following convenient list in the *Bible-Science Newsletter* (November, 1975):

1. Only man employs a propositional language, only man uses verbal symbols, only man makes sentences; i.e., only man is a discursive animal.
2. Only man makes tools, builds fires, erects shelters, fabricates clothing, i.e., only man is a technological animal.

3. Only man enacts laws or sets up his own rules of behavior and thereby constitutes his social life, organizing his association with his fellows in a variety of different ways, i.e., only man is a political, not just a gregarious animal.

4. Only man has developed, in the course of generations, a cumulative cultural tradition, the transmission of which constitutes human history, i.e., only man is a historical animal.

5. Only man engages in magical ritualistic practices, i.e., only man is a religious animal.

6. Only man has a moral conscience, a sense of right and wrong, and of values, i.e., only man is an ethical animal.

7. Only man decorates or adorns himself or his artifacts, and makes pictures or statues for the non-utilitarian purpose or enjoyment, i.e. only man is an esthetic animal.

Man has unique traits that distinguish him from other animals and this evidence agrees with God's revealed Word.

Appendix II

The following reading list is taken from *Scientific Creationism,* prepared by the technical staff and consultants of the Institute for Creation Research; edited by Henry M. Morris (San Diego, Calif.: Creation-Life Publishers, 1974).

Bibliography on Creationism

The books and periodicals listed below are recommended for all school libraries in order to provide students and teachers access to a fair sample of the available literature on scientific creationism. All books listed are believed to be currently in print.

I.   *Books by creationist scientists emphasizing the scientific aspects of creationism.*

*Barnes, Thomas G., *Origin and Destiny of the Earth's Magnetic Field* (San Diego: Institute for Creation Research, 1973), 64 pp.

Clark, Robert E.D., *Darwin: Before and After* (Chicago: Moody Press, 1967), 192 pp.

Clark, Harold W., *Fossils, Flood and Fire* (Escondido, Calif.: Outdoor Pictures, 1968), 239 pp.

Cook, Melvin A., *Prehistory and Earth Models* (London: Max Parrish Co., 1966), 353 pp.

Coppedge, James, *Evolution: Possible or Impossible?* (Grand Rapids: Zondervan, 1973), 276 pp.

Cousins, Frank W., *Fossil Man* (Hants, England: Evolution Protest Movement, 1966), 106 pp.

Daly, Reginald, *Earth's Most Challenging Mysteries* (Nutley, N.J.: Craig Press, 1972), 403 pp.

Davidheiser, Bolton, *Evolution and Christian Faith* (Nutley, N.J.: Presbyterian and Reformed Publ. Co., 1969), 372 pp.

Dewar, Douglas, *The Transformist Illusion* (Murfreesboro, Tenn.: DeHoff Publ., 1955), 306 pp.

Enoch, H., *Evolution or Creation* (Madras, Union of Evangelical Students of India, 1966), 172 pp.

Friar, Wayne & Wm. P. Davis, *The Case for Creation* (Chicago: Moody Press, 1972), 93 pp.

*Gish, Duane T., *Speculations and Experiments on the Origin of Life* (San Diego: Institute for Creation Research, 1972), 41 pp.

*Gish, Duane T., *Evolution: The Fossils Say No!* (San Diego: Institute for Creation Research, 1973), 144 pp.

Klotz, John W., *Genes, Genesis and Evolution* (St. Louis: Concordia, 1970), 544 pp.

*Lammerts, W.E. (Ed.), *Why Not Creation?* (Philadelphia: Presbyterian and Reformed Co., 1970), 388 pp.

*Lammerts, W.E. (Ed.), *Scientific Studies in Special Creation* (Philadelphia: Presbyterian and Reformed Co., 1971), 343 pp.

Marsh, Frank L., *Life, Man and Time* (Escondido, Calif.: Outdoor Pictures, 1967), 238 pp.

*Moore, John N. and Harold S. Slusher (Eds.), *Biology: A Search for Order in Complexity* (2nd Edition, Grand Rapids: Zondervan, 1974, 595 pp.

*Morris, Henry M. and John C. Whitcomb, *The Genesis Flood* (Philadelphia: Presbyterian and Reformed Co., 1961), 518 pp.

*Morris, Henry M., *The Twilight of Evolution* (Grand Rapids: Baker Book House, 1964), 103 pp.

*Morris, Henry M., Wm. W. Boardman, and Robert F. Koontz, *Science and Creation* (San Diego: Creation-Science Research Center, 1971), 98 pp.

Morris, Henry M. et al, *A Symposium on Creation* (Grand Rapids: Baker Book House, 1968), 156 pp.

Patten, Donald W. (Ed.), *Symposium on Creation II* (Grand Rapids: Baker Book House, 1970), 151 pp.

Patten, Donald W. (Ed.), *Symposium on Creation III* (Grand Rapids: Baker Book House, 1971), 150 pp.

Patten, Donald W. (Ed.), *Symposium on Creation IV* (Grand Rapids: Baker Book House, 1972), 159 pp.

Shute, Evan, *Flaws in the Theory of Evolution* (Philadelphia: Presbyterian and Reformed Co., 1966), 286 pp.

Siegler, H.R., *Evolution or Degeneration—Which?* (Milwaukee: Northwestern Publishing House, 1972), 128 pp.

*Slusher, Harold S., *Critique of Radiometric Dating* (San Diego: Institute for Creation Research, 1973), 46 pp.

Smith, A.E. Wilder, *Man's Origin, Man's Destiny* (Wheaton, Illinois: Harold Shaw Co., 1968), 320 pp.

Smith, A.E. Wilder, *The Creation of Life* (Wheaton, Illinois: Harold Shaw Publishers, 1970), 269 pp.

Tinkle, William J., *Heredity* (Grand Rapids: Zondervan, 1970), 182 pp.

Utt, Richard H. (Ed.), *Creation: Nature's Designs and Designer* (Mountain View, Calif.: Pacific Press, 1971), 182 pp.

Zimmerman, Paul A. (Ed.), *Darwin, Evolution and Creation* (St. Louis: Concordia Publ. House, 1959), 231 pp.

II. *Books by evolutionists containing valuable critiques of aspects of evolutionary theory or practice.*

Barzun, Jacques, *Darwin, Marx, Wagner* (New York: Doubleday, 1958), 373 pp.

Blum, Harold F. *Time's Arrow and Evolution* (Princeton: Princeton University Press, 1962), 224 pp.

Haller, John S., *Outcasts from Evolution* (Urbana: University of Illinois, 1971), 228 pp.

Heribert-Nilsson, N., *Synthetische Artbildung* (An English summary) (Victoria, B.C.: Evolutionist Protest Movement, 1973).

Himmelfarb, Gertrude, *Darwin and the Darwinian*

Revolution (London: Chatto and Windus, 1959), 422 pp.

Keith, Arthur, *Evolution and Ethics* (New York: Putnam, 1947), 239 pp.

Kerkut, G.A., *Implications of Evolution* (London: Pergamon Press, 1960), 174 pp.

MacBeth, Norman, *Darwin Retried* (Boston: Gambit, Inc., 1971), 172 pp.

Matthews, L. Harrison, *Introduction to "Origin of Species"* (London: J. M. Dent & Sons, Ltd., 1971).

Moorhead, P.S. and M. M. Kaplan (Eds.), *Mathematical Challenges to the Neo-Darwinian Interpretation of Evolution* (Philadelphia: Wistar Institute Press, 1967), 140 pp.

Salet, G., *Hasard et Certitude* (Paris: Tequi-Diffusion, 1972), 456 pp.

Zirkle, Conway, *Evolution, Marxian Biology, and the Social Scene* (Philadelphia: University of Pennsylvania Press, 1959), 527 pp.

III. *Books by creationist authors, both scientists and theologians, discussing relation between science and the Bible.*

Clark, R.T. and James D. Bales, *Why Scientists Accept Evolution* (Nutley, N.J.: Presbyterian and Reformed Publ. Co., 1966), 113 pp.

Coder, S. Maxwell and George F. Howe, *The Bible, Science and Creation* (Chicago: Moody Press, 1965), 128 pp.

*Morris, Henry M., *Many Infallible Proofs* (San Diego: Creation-Life Publishers, 1974), 386 pp.

*Morris, Henry M., *Evolution and the Modern Christian* (Philadelphia: Presbyterian and Reformed Publ. Co., 1967), 72 pp.

*Morris, Henry M., *The Remarkable Birth of Planet Earth* (San Diego: Institute for Creation Research, 1972), 114 pp.

*Morris, Henry M., *Science, Scripture and Salvation* (Denver: Baptist Publications, 1971), 155 pp.

*Morris, Henry M., *Biblical Cosmology and Modern Science* (Nutley, N.J.: Craig Press, 1970), 146 pp.

*Morris, Henry M., *Studies in the Bible and Science* (Philadelphia: Presbyterian and Reformed Co., 1966), 186 pp.

*Morris, Henry M., *The Bible and Modern Science* (Chicago: Moody Press, 1968), 128 pp.

Nelson, Byron C., *The Deluge Story in Stone* (Minneapolis: Bethany Fellowship, 1968), 204 pp.

Rehwinkel, Alfred A., *The Flood* (St. Louis: Concordia, 1951), 372 pp.

Rushdoony, Rousas J., *The Mythology of Science* (Nutley, N.J.: Craig Press, 1967), 134 pp.

*Schnabel, A. O., *Has God Spoken?* (San Diego: Creation-Life Publishers, 1974), 118 pp.

Tinkle, William J., *God's Method in Creation* (Nutley, N.J.: Craig Press, 1973), 93 pp.

*Whitcomb, John C., *Origin of the Solar System* (Nutley, N.J.: Presbyterian and Reformed Publ. Co., 1964), 34 pp.

*Whitcomb, John C., *The Early Earth* (Nutley, N.J.: Craig Press, 1972), 144 pp.

*Whitcomb, John C., *The World That Perished* (Grand Rapids: Baker Book House, 1973), 155 pp.

*Woods, Andrew J., *The Center of the Earth* (San Diego: Institute for Creation Research, 1973), 18 pp.

*Available from Creation-Life Publishers, P.O. Box 15666, San Diego, CA 92115.

Recommended Periodicals

Acts and Facts (San Diego, Institute for Creation Research, published monthly).

Creation Research Quarterly (Ann Arbor, Michigan, Creation Research Society, published quarterly).

Doorway Papers (Ottawa, Arthur C. Custance, published as ready).

Bible-Science Newsletter (Caldwell, Idaho, Bible-Science Association, published monthly).

E.P.M. Papers (Hayling Island, Hants, England, Evolution Protest Movement, published as ready).

Addenda to preceding reading list:

Morris, Henry M., ed., *Scientific Creationism* (San Diego: Creation-Life Publishers, 1974).

Rimmer, Harry, *Dead Men Tell Tales* (Grand Rapids: Eerdmans, 1939).

Rimmer, Harry, *The Harmony of Science and Scripture* (Grand Rapids: Eerdmans, 1936).

Rimmer, Harry, *The Magnificence of Jesus* (Grand Rapids: Eerdmans, 1943).

Rimmer, Harry, *Modern Science and the Genesis Record* (Grand Rapids: Eerdmans, 1937).

Rimmer, Harry, *Theory of Evolution and the Facts of Science* (Grand Rapids: Eerdmans, 1935).

Appendix III

A Few Scientific Facts the Bible Knew Before the Scientists Caught On

Evolution is impossible, because every seed reproduces its own genus:

> And the earth brought forth grass, and herb yielding *seed after his kind,* and the tree yielding fruit, whose seed was in itself, *after his kind. . . .* And God created great whales, and every living creature that moveth, which the waters brought forth abundantly, *after their kind,* and every winged fowl *after his kind. . . .* And God said, Let the earth bring forth the living creature *after his kind,* cattle and creeping thing, and the beast of the earth *after his kind* (Genesis 1:12, 21, 24).

There is great wealth in the sea:

The abundant wealth of the Dead Sea shall be turned to you (Isaiah 60:5 TAB).

[A footnote in the Amplified Bible explains:

Prior to well in the twentieth century, scholars could only speculate as to what Isaiah could have meant here by "the abundant wealth of the sea" that was one day to be turned over to Jerusalem. . . . The Dead Sea for ages had been considered only a place of death and desolation. . . . Then suddenly it was discovered that the waters of the Dead Sea contained important chemicals. In 1935 A.D., G.T.B. Davis wrote in his *Rebuilding Palestine,* "One is almost staggered by the computed wealth of the chemical salts in the Dead Sea. It is estimated that the potential value of the potash, bromine, and other chemical salts of the waters is . . . four times the wealth of the United States!" Isaiah himself did not know this, but the God who made the Dead Sea for a part in His end-time program knew all about it, and caused this record to say so.]

Light involves motion:

Where is the *way* where light dwells? (Job 38:19 TAB).

[Here again, the Amplified Bible explains:

How, except by divine inspiration, could Job have known that light does not dwell in a *place,* but a *way*? For light, as modern man has discovered, involves motion, wave motion, and traveling 186,000 miles a second, it can only dwell in a way.]

There are currents in the ocean:

The birds of the air, and the fish of the sea, and whatever passes along the *paths of the seas* (Psalm 8:8 TAB).

There is a hydrographic circulatory system on this planet:

> Who calls for the waters of the sea, and pours them out upon
> the face of the earth? (Amos 5:8 TAB).

There is music coming from the stars, now detectable by scientific instruments as a shrill, creaking sound:

> When the morning stars sang together (Job 38:7 TAB).

There is an infinite number of stars:

> As the host of heaven cannot be numbered (Jeremiah 33:22).

[Human wisdom had said, "There are exactly 1026 stars" (Hipparchus 150 B.C.); "The total of the stars is 1056" (Ptolemy, at the time of Christ); "They can't be numbered" (Galileo A.D. 1610, looking through a telescope).]

The stars are not pure:

> Yea, the stars are not pure in his sight (Job 25:5).

[The ancient notion that the stars are pure was first refuted by Galileo when he observed sun spots through the telescope.]

High explosives can be safely shipped in shaved ice:

> Hast thou entered into the treasures of the snow? Or hast thou seen the treasures of the hail which I have reserved against the time of trouble, against the day of battle and war? (Job 38:22-23).

[During World War I, we were having trouble controlling high explosives. They were being detonated by the ship's motion. A Jewish scientist who sought God for the answer to the problem was given the directive, "Pack them in shaved ice." It solved the problem.]

The first law of thermodynamics is that nothing is being created or destroyed:

> Thus the heavens and the earth were finished, and all the host of them (Genesis 2:1). But by the same word the present heavens and earth have been stored up (reserved) for fire, being kept until the day of judgment . . . (II Peter 3:7).

Write today for your sample copies of

 **LOGOS**JOURNAL

North America's largest charismatic magazine

and

NATIONAL COURIER

the exciting new tabloid

accurately reporting and commenting on news

of the world with a Christian perspective

Name _____

Address _____

City _____ State _____ Zip _____

☐ Send me a sample copy of *Logos Journal*
☐ Send me a sample copy of the *National Courier*

*(Please enclose 50 cents per sample for
handling and shipping)*